To Monic
Hovillet.......

dreams
visions
AND THEIR
INTERPRETATIONS

Pastor Uzor Ndekwu

dreams
visions
AND THEIR
INTERPRETATIONS

Pastor Uzor Ndekwu

United Kingdom:

Uzor Ndekwu Ministries (Jesus Sanctuary)
25/27 Ruby Street
Old Kent Road
London SE15 1LR
United Kingdom
Tel: +44 207 277 5664; +44 7961 276 187
Email: info@jesussanctuaryministries.org
Website: www.jesussanctuaryministries.org

Nigeria:

Uzor Ndekwu Ministries (Jesus Sanctuary)
41 Otigba Crescent
GRA
Onitsha
Anambra State
Nigeria
Te: +234 803 395 0197; +234 803 405 2113

Published by:

Uzor Ndekwu Ministries (Jesus Sanctuary)

Copyright© Uzor Ndekwu 2018

Bible quotations are from the King James Version of the Holy Bible.

Printed by

Memoirs Publishers
England

ISBN 978-1-86151-886-6

dreams visions AND THEIR INTERPRETATIONS

CONTENTS

Acknowledgements

I wish to express my profound thanks to the following persons: my wife for her informed comments and contributions towards the editing of this book; Sister Josephine Ife for the revision of the first part of this book, originally, *Dreams and Visions*; Brother Colin Ife and Sister Amara Chukwuenweniwe for their contributions towards the second part of this book, including revising and editing the extensive symbols, interpretations, and the included prayer points; and to Ms. Kelly Moody for the editing and proofreading of this book.

Introduction

I am delighted to offer this Second Edition of *Dreams and Visions* under the new title *Dreams, Visions, and Their Interpretations.*

Dreams and visions are powerful insights into the impact of the spiritual realm on the physical realm. People dream and either ignore them out of ignorance or turn to the wrong channels for interpretation, often with disastrous consequences.

From my own personal family experience as a deliverance pastor and biblical counsellor and also through my interactive telecasts, I have come to realise the significance of dreams and visions and their correct interpretations. This is the subject of the first edition of my book *Dreams and Visions*, published in 2007. It focused on the power, role, meanings, types, conditions, revelations, interpretations, and important tips on dreams and visions.

Following feedback from numerous readers, it became imperative that I enlighten Christendom and the world at large on the interpretation of dreams and visions, as there is a heightened demand for it. In order to be effective as a Christian, it is not enough to dream or see visions; it is their interpretation that points to the correct actions necessary to forestall the plan of the enemy. Interpretation is also what gives insight into the message or direction the Lord is giving to the individual concerned. There are levels of dreams and visions and principal ways and methods that God speaks to us. It is therefore important that we decode and interpret God's messages accurately.

The principal innovation of this Second Edition is the focus on interpretations. It is not just to reorganise the existing material, based on the first edition, but also to introduce new depths, which reflect additional insights into the realm of dreams and visions since the First Edition was published. Extensive situational and contextual analyses, as well as relevant biblical references, are provided to broaden your understanding of interpretations, hence the revised title of the book: *Dreams, Visions, and Their Interpretations.*

I am humbled by the immense support given me by all who researched and provided material for this piece of revelation. I am extremely grateful to the editor and all who played a role in bringing to life this Second Edition. Your dint of hard work will certainly not go unrecognised by our God.

PART I

Chapter 1

The Power of Dreams and Visions

In both the church and the world today, there is a renewed zeal and hunger for the supernatural. This zeal stems from an increasing need for spiritual guidance in our complex world.

The desire to accomplish God's purposes for our lives ought to be a consuming passion for all. For God's purpose for us is for good and not for evil, enabling us to achieve our expected goal and end (Jeremiah 29:11).

When God created us, He designed us for a purpose; you were born to be unique. We all have a different genetic makeup: our fingerprints, blood type, eye colour, and even psychological dispositions are unique. God's blueprint and roadmap for your life are eternally determined. Ephesians 1:4 says:

1

"According as he hath chosen us in him before the foundation of the world, that we should be holy and without blame before him in love."

All of creation, the heavens and the earth, you and I, are products of vision. Before God created us, He saw us in His mind's eye, as evidenced in His words to Jeremiah:

"Before I formed thee in the belly I knew thee; and before thou camest forth out of the womb I sanctified thee, and I ordained thee a prophet unto the nations" (Jeremiah 1:5).

Because we are created in God's image and likeness (Genesis 1:26–27), we also have the Power of Vision, which can take the form of dreams and, literally, visions in our mind's eye. We are the only creation of God that is tripartite — spirit, soul, and body. We receive these dreams and visions through the operation of our spirit-man.

Although mankind was created with the Power of Revelation in the Garden of Eden, Adam communicated with God face-to-face, and there was no barrier; the flesh was neither weak nor sinful. This, however, was no longer the case after the Fall. From Genesis 3 onwards, sin became a barrier (Isaiah 59:2), and the sinful flesh of man had to be bypassed. Exodus 33:20 says, **"for there shall no man see me, and live."** As a result, God communicates with mankind by the Power of Revelation through dreams and visions.

Original sin caused man's "spiritual eye of understanding" to be closed while his "physical eye of understanding" was opened (Genesis 3:5–7). Man now began to reason and understand from the soulish and physical realms instead of the spiritual realm, which should control these two. Thus, many errors of judgment and discernment have occurred throughout history. We cannot afford to ignore this dimension of revelation, as God uses it to communicate with mankind to prevent, redress, or show this nature of errors. We ignore this dimension at our own peril.

Scripture is clear that each one of us is a product of revelation and vision. In the same way, as children made in the image of God, manifestations of revelation in the forms of visions, trances, and dreams are meant to be normal occurrences in our lives. The Bible says that we are to desire such revelation earnestly:

> **"Now concerning spiritual gifts, brethren, I would not have you ignorant... For to one is given by the Spirit the word of wisdom; to another the word of knowledge by the same Spirit; To another faith by the same Spirit; To another the gifts of healing by the same Spirit; To another the working of miracles; to another prophecy; to another discerning of spirits"** (1 Corinthians 12:1, 8–10).

In these last days, God's wish is for all His children to be dreamers, visionaries, and decoders of the supernatural. For God knows that you need to understand the spiritual realm if you are to achieve your purpose in life. The realm of the unseen rules the visible realm (2 Corinthians 4:18). How many lives, marriages, businesses, and ministries could have been saved if such revelations from God were taken more seriously? I strongly believe that if many people knew the meaning of their dreams or visions, their lives would be completely different. Revelation from God can come through different means:

- Dreams
- Visions
- Trances
- Out-of-body experiences
- Face-to-face communication with God

For the purposes of this book, our primary focus will be on dreams and visions. However, in order that your understanding may be broadened and made clear, I shall go ahead and define all the terms referred to above.

DREAMS

Everybody dreams — saints and sinners alike. Dreams always come in our state of sleep. Nebuchadnezzar in Daniel 4:4–18 and Jacob in Genesis 28:11–15 both had dreams that were from God. However, as well as being messages and revelations from God, dreams can originate from the heavenlies, whether angelic or satanic, or come about as a result of psycho-emotional experiences in relation to our environment. For example, someone in constant conflict with a colleague may dream that he/she is in a fight with that colleague.

VISIONS

Visions occur in our conscious or semi-conscious state and are a higher level of revelation than dreams. They come about only when one's heart and mind are completely attuned to God. Abraham in Genesis 15:1, Daniel in Daniel 2:19, and Paul in Acts 18:9 all received visions from God that they heeded and obeyed.

TRANCES

A trance has to do with the conditions under which a vision is seen. Here, the consciousness and perception of natural circumstances are suppressed and a person's spirit is in tune only with the spiritual realm. One can see what God is revealing without the interference of the body or soul. In Acts 10:9–16, for example, Peter became very hungry and was about to eat when he fell into a trance.

OUT-OF-BODY EXPERIENCE

Out-of-body experiences occur when a man's spirit is literally transported out of his body by the Spirit of God and taken to another realm to be shown certain spiritual or even physical events. In Ezekiel 37, God showed Ezekiel the true spiritual state of Israel using the valley of the dry bones as a metaphor. Paul also talks about how he was caught up in Paradise in 2 Corinthians 12:2–4.

FACE-TO-FACE COMMUNICATION

As earlier indicated, this form of communication existed between man (Adam and Eve) and God before the fall of man. Sequel to the Fall, this form of communication has become rare and exceptional. Only a deep level of relationship with God can enable someone to have this sort of revelation. Moses, for example, enjoyed that kind of relationship with God and so experienced this form of communication (Exodus 33:11–30 and Numbers 12:8).

These forms of revelations are part of the spiritual gifts found in 1 Corinthians 12:1–8:

> **"Now concerning spiritual gifts, brethren, I would not have you ignorant… For to one is given by the Spirit the word of wisdom; to another the word of knowledge by the same Spirit."**

The Bible makes it clear that as God pours out His Spirit upon us in the last days, there will be an increase in dreams, visions, and other revelations. As it says in Joel 2:28–29 and Acts 2:17–18,

"And it shall come to pass in the last days, saith God, I will pour out of my Spirit upon all flesh: and your sons and your daughters shall prophesy, and your young men shall see visions, and your old men shall dream dreams: And on my servants and on my handmaidens I will pour out in those days of my Spirit; and they shall prophesy."

We need to covet these gifts and have a greater desire for their manifestations in these turbulent times. We need to understand what is operating in the spiritual realm if we are to fulfil our destiny. The unseen or spiritual realm rules the seen or physical realm, but through revelation, it is made known to us. The truth, therefore, is that revelations such as dreams and visions are not optional but a necessity if we are to take charge of events in our lives.

From the Bible, we see that God uses revelation to explain the natural as it relates to our current situation, future disposition, or even eternity. In the womb of these dreams and visions lies a promise to be manifested, a puzzle waiting to be revealed, or a warning to be heeded. Jesus' own life was preserved through dreams when God exposed Herod's intention to kill Him to the wise men and Joseph (Matthew 2).

In the Old Testament (Genesis 37), the destiny of Joseph, son of Jacob, was shown through dreams and helped him in the difficult times before the fulfilment of God's promise. In Genesis 41, Pharaoh's dream was a puzzle to explain, yet with the help of Joseph, Egypt and neighbouring countries were saved from dying of starvation.

Many people have gone astray and suffered unnecessarily because they did not understand their revelations. Scripture says that God's people perish for lack of knowledge (Hosea 4:6). Many have missed opportunities because they did not take their dreams seriously. Just as Pharaoh, Nebuchadnezzar, and Daniel did not cast aside their dreams and visions but sought interpretations and solutions, so should we. Unfortunately, because little has been said in Christendom about dreams and visions, many spiritually hungry and ignorant people are drawn to false prophets, mystics, psychics, mediums, and astrologers to explain what only God can rightly interpret. Jeremiah lamented:

> **"Behold, I am against them that prophesy false dreams, saith the LORD, and do tell them, and cause my people to err by their lies, and by their lightness; yet I sent them not, nor commanded them: therefore they shall not profit this people at all, saith the LORD" (Jeremiah 23:32).**

There are television networks and communication outlets devoted to psychic and mystic revelations. No doubt, these are demonic and meant to promote evil practices that open people up to occultism and ungodly influences. God is highly displeased when we seek revelation by any of these means.

"There shall not be found among you any one that maketh his son or his daughter to pass through the fire, or that useth divination, or an observer of times, or an enchanter, or a witch, Or a charmer, or a consulter with familiar spirits, or a wizard, or a necromancer. For all that do these things are an abomination unto the LORD: and because of these abominations the LORD thy God doth drive them out from before thee" (Deuteronomy 18:10–12).

A revelation may be true, but it may not have come from God. Paul was troubled by a girl with a gift of divination. What she was saying was true, but the source was demonic.

"And it came to pass, as we went to prayer, a certain damsel possessed with a spirit of divination met us, which brought her masters much gain by soothsaying: The same followed Paul and us, and cried, saying, These men are the servants of the most high God, which shew unto us the way of salvation. And this did she many days. But Paul, being grieved, turned and said to the spirit, I command thee in the name of Jesus Christ to come out of her. And he came out the same hour" Acts 16:16–18).

We are not to seek these means as King Saul did:

> **"And when Saul enquired of the LORD, the LORD answered him not, neither by dreams, nor by Urim, nor by prophets. Then said Saul unto his servants, Seek me a woman that hath a familiar spirit, that I may go to her, and enquire of her. And his servants said to him, Behold, there is a woman that hath a familiar spirit at Endor"** (1 Samuel 28:6–7).

God says,

> **"My people are destroyed for lack of knowledge: because thou hast rejected knowledge, I will also reject thee"** (Hosea 4:6).

Because of a lack of knowledge of revelation, many are perplexed, confused, and frustrated. We need genuine, truth-based knowledge to be able to apply it to our lives. This verse suggests that those who constantly reject revelation as psycho-emotional and reject the knowledge are less likely to fulfil the purposes that God has for them.

In the next chapter, we shall look in detail at dreams and visions.

Chapter 2

Different Kinds of Dreams and Visions

Dreams and visions are either carnal or spiritual. Dreams occur in our state of sleep, while visions are usually in our conscious state.

DREAMS

Carnal Dreams

Carnal dreams result from activities, emotions, thoughts, physical experiences, and contacts that become embedded in our subconsciousness throughout the day. At night, these images, ideas, and hopes begin to play themselves out in the form of dreams. For example, the strong passion with the soulish realm of an individual will show up in dreams. The content of such dreams exposes our will, emotions, and intellectual disposition over a matter. The power of our imagination also gives rise to carnal dreams. Scripture says:

> **"It shall even be as when an hungry man dreameth, and, behold, he eateth; but he awaketh, and his soul is empty: or as when a thirsty man dreameth, and, behold, he drinketh; but he awaketh, and, behold, he is faint, and his soul hath appetite: so shall the multitude of all the nations be, that fight against mount Zion"** (Isaiah 29:8).

Elsewhere it says:

> **"For in the multitude of dreams and many words there are also divers vanities: but fear thou God"** (Ecclesiastes 5:7).

As a pastor, I have come across several cases during times of counselling for which I will like to share a few.

Case One: Rosemary (not her real name) came to see me because she had a problem with finding a life partner. She felt that God had shown her the man she was to marry in several dreams. Yet, she could not understand how this man had been God's choice for her. Obviously, God does not make mistakes. After posing a lot of questions and dialoguing with her, it became evident that she was getting on in age and was, therefore, desperate to marry. As a result, she had developed a strong desire and emotional attachment to this man, which resulted in her dreams about him. The dreams were not from God but rather her soulish passions.

Case Two: A woman in her early twenties complained about making love to strange men in her sleep. Sometimes, this is a demonic attack, but I soon found out that in her own case, it was not so. She lived a sexually immoral life and enjoyed pornographic films and magazines. These images became embedded in her soul and were manifested in her dreams at night.

Case Three: A middle-aged man told me that he regularly dreamed that he was always quarrelling with his neighbour. Sometimes, the quarrel led to physical fights. It turned out that he and his neighbour were not on good terms and had never got on very well. The hostility in his heart towards his neighbour was manifesting in his dreams.

There is a well-known computing term "GIGO," meaning "garbage in, garbage out." In other words, whatever we feed on will show up in the final result. That is the case in every part of our lives. When we fill our lives with garbage from violent, sexually immoral and evil books, films, activities, and discussions, they become embedded in the soul (will, mind, emotions). Subsequently, when we sleep, these implantations and embodiments in our souls arise in our unconscious state and play out in our dreams.

SPIRITUAL DREAMS

Spiritual dreams are channels of communication between the heavenlies and the natural or physical realm. Every spiritual dream is either a message (promise, information, encouragement, or warning) from God or an exposure of the plots, plans, and purposes of demonic forces in the heavenly places.

> **"For we wrestle not against flesh and blood, but against principalities, against powers, against the rulers of the darkness of this world, against spiritual wickedness in high places"** (Ephesians 6:12).

Through spiritual dreams, unseen forces can break effortlessly into the physical or natural realm. God speaks to both believers and unbelievers alike through this means. In Daniel 4:4–5, we read:

> **"I Nebuchadnezzar was at rest in mine house, and flourishing in my palace: I saw a dream which made me afraid, and the thoughts upon my bed and the visions of my head troubled me."**

Other examples include:

> **"But God came to Abimelech in a dream by night, and said to him, Behold, thou art but a dead man, for the woman which thou hast taken; for she is a man's wife"** (Genesis 20:3).

"And it came to pass at the end of two full years, that Pharaoh dreamed: and, behold, he stood by the river" (Genesis 41:1).

"But while he thought on these things, behold, the angel of the Lord appeared unto him in a dream, saying, Joseph, thou son of David, fear not to take unto thee Mary thy wife: for that which is conceived in her is of the Holy Ghost" (Matthew 1:20).

"When he was set down on the judgment seat, his wife sent unto him, saying, Have thou nothing to do with that just man: for I have suffered many things this day in a dream because of him" (Matthew 27:19).

In my own life, God has used dreams to guide me and expose secret things to me. In 1995, I dreamed that I was preaching in crusades; many souls were saved, the sick were healed, and the dead were raised to life. At the time, I was still a "baby Christian." I had no formal role in the church and was still working full-time in a bank. Four years later, while still working in a bank, I became an assistant pastor and what I had seen in the dream began to come to pass. Seven years after the dream, when I entered full-time ministry on my own, I began to hold crusades with many souls being saved and the sick, healed. Several people have been raised to life, and I am still expecting greater miracles to happen with the help of the Holy Spirit.

Before I went into full-time ministry in August 2001, God showed me in a dream that I would leave the ministry where I was an assistant pastor and also gave me the exact exit date of 14th April 2002. The separation occurred just as God had told me it would, and my ministry took off.

Another example I would like to share was when I became a full-time pastor. A month later, God showed me that all the ministers working with me would leave and be replaced by new ones. I could not envisage how this would be possible because they all seemed loyal and hard-working; however, I was convicted that God does not lie. Only God knows the heart of man, and He alone can expose it.

"The heart is deceitful above all things, and desperately wicked: who can know it? I the LORD search the heart, I try the reins, even to give every man according to his ways, and according to the fruit of his doings" (Jeremiah 17:9–10).

I looked at the outward appearance, examining their hard work and commitment to my ministry, but God saw their hearts and knew that they could not work for long in the ministry. Within a span of two years, they had all left the ministry. Let us be conscious of God's words in 1 Samuel 16:7:

"But the LORD said unto Samuel, Look not on his countenance, or on the height of his

stature; because I have refused him: for the LORD seeth not as man seeth; for man looketh on the outward appearance, but the LORD looketh on the heart."

There were other times after this when God exposed workers who outwardly appeared committed to the ministry but, in reality, were wolves in sheep clothing. A lady who joined our church in 1999 seemed to be a great asset to the ministry, as she was disciplined, hard-working, and discharged her duties with utmost attention. Doors that seemed closed began to open for her as she worked towards achieving the goals set out for her. She was highly respected and appeared to be a wonderful Christian role model. God, however, who sees the heart, kept on revealing her as a witch not only to myself but also to my wife and other members of the church. We could not reconcile what we were seeing in our dreams with what we could see with our natural eyes. The spiritual world, however, is the real world, and God exposed the intents and diabolical desires of her heart. After a while, she began to manifest what God had revealed to us, including the evil plots and plans she had to bring down the ministry. Eventually, she left as a result of a vision, which I will explain in depth as I talk about visions.

One night, I dreamed of a rat running around our altar. God revealed to me that it represented one of the ministers in the church who was dishonest. As with the other cases, I found it hard to accept that this apparently loyal, encouraging, and hard-working man was stealing and lying about church finances. He seemed most aggrieved anytime someone cheated the ministry even by a negligible margin, yet he was embezzling our funds. God ultimately exposed him, and he left the church.

Even before I became a Christian, when I was in the university, God revealed to me all my examination questions in a dream. It resulted in me coming out with exceptional grades in my courses. I received both federal and state scholarships as a result of this and emerged the best student in my department.

Unfortunately, as a nominal Christian, I did not always heed the warnings that God gave me through dreams, and thus, I learned a very painful lesson in life. God warned me about the death of my elder brother in a dream several months before he died, but I did not take it seriously. I dreamed that I saw both his son and myself dressed in black. We were receiving pension benefits from his employer and our faces were gloomy and sad. I told my brother the dream, and we laughed and joked about it together. Eight months down the line, he was diagnosed with cancer of the pancreas and died shortly afterwards. His death had a serious impact on me, and I became born again. I realised that God shows us things in our dreams so that we can act on them. I knew that if I had been a committed Christian, I would have entered a period of fasting and prayer to avert the calamity. In a later chapter, I will elaborate more on how warnings from God should be handled and how plots and plans from the wicked one can be averted.

So many dreams that I have had have given me direction, necessary information, warnings about somebody or something or even sometimes, my very own self. They have been a source of encouragement and have revealed my destiny, gifts, and also aspects of God hitherto undiscovered by me. Before I moved to my current home, it was revealed to me in a dream. The same occurred with my home in Nigeria. Many dangers and evil have been averted simply by paying attention to dreams. God will usually reveal just a glimpse of something sinister happening in the spiritual realm as a way of cautioning us.

Our dreams are important, and we should not take them for granted or cast them away. Thank God for His Word and His Holy Spirit that teach and guide us through life.

VISIONS

This is the next level of revelation, which is much higher than dreams. Everybody dreams, but not everybody has visions. There are many types of visions, and these can be either carnal or spiritual.

Carnal Visions

Carnal visions, just like carnal dreams, are socio-emotionally stimulated or derived from the soulish realm. They may be linked to an inner witness or conviction concerning a set of ideas or goals over social, economic, environmental, or other factors.

To achieve greatness in this world, you must have a vision and set goals. A vision can push you to excel and to achieve great things in the face of current obstacles, adverse situations, negative reactions from others, the lack of talent, as well as a financial or social provision. Great historical figures such as Martin Luther King Jr., Nelson Mandela, Mahatma Gandhi, Mother Theresa, Esther in the Bible, General William Booth of the Salvation Army Movement, John Bunyan, and Abraham Lincoln were all motivated to bring about change in this world because of the evil they witnessed. They visualised the ideal situation and began to work towards it. They did not allow failure, lack, or any other "impossibility" to keep them from fulfilling their vision.

Carnal visions are different from carnal dreams in that they have sustained people, activated good movements, and caused a lot of good and greatness to be achieved. Carnal dreams, on the other hand, only show our state of mind and are of little use to anyone. The Bible says in Proverbs 29:18:

"Where there is no vision, the people perish: but he that keepeth the law, happy is he."

The NIV translation puts it this way:

"Where there is no revelation, people cast off restraint."

In other words, without a clear vision, people become purposeless and wander around with no sense of direction.

They cast off restraint, that is to say, they ignore moral standards and begin to live a life of crime and sin, accepting all evil going on around them. Nothing restrains them from opposing the Will of God.

Carnal visions are a must for every human being. Without them, you will never achieve anything worthwhile in this world. The God that created us is a God of vision. He visualised His creation before He spoke it into being. He is a God of purpose and plan, and since we are made in His image, we must also be people of vision, purpose, and plan.

In Jeremiah 29:11, God said:

"For I know the thoughts that I think toward you, saith the LORD, thoughts of peace, and not of evil, to give you an expected end."

Unfortunately, only a few people are focused on life and have a specific vision or set goals concerning their future.

Samson in Judges 13–16 is a good example. Despite the wonderful plans God had for him and the purpose for which he was born, he lived a careless and directionless life. He was anointed for God's plan and purpose but had no vision of why he was called. He rather chose to use his anointing to settle personal scores (Judges 14:19; 15:4–5, 7–8; 15:14–19; 16:1–4) or to show off (Judges 14:5–6). In light of this, a man destined for greatness and having such enviable potential ended up in the hands of his enemies, a defeated and disgraced man.

The children of Israel in the wilderness were unable to

enter the promised land, even though they were able to do so, because they had lost sight of their collective vision. That generation died in the wilderness (Numbers 13:28–32 and Numbers 14:1–30).

It is, however, not enough to have a vision; we must follow it through by making it clear and setting goals to achieve it.

> **"And the LORD answered me, and said, Write the vision, and make it plain upon tables, that he may run that readeth it. For the vision is yet for an appointed time, but at the end it shall speak, and not lie: though it tarry, wait for it; because it will surely come, it will not tarry"** (Habakkuk 2:2–3).

Do not allow your perception of the natural to derail you from your vision. Natural talents, human support, social contacts, finances, wisdom, and so on are all good but not an absolute guarantee of success in themselves. For when we have a vision, all that we need to fulfil it will come. The Preacher in Ecclesiastes 9:11 says:

> **"I returned, and saw under the sun, that the race is not to the swift, nor the battle to the strong, neither yet bread to the wise, nor yet riches to men of understanding, nor yet favour to men of skill; but time and chance happeneth to them all."**

Time, circumstances, friends, family, relations, social and economic policies may fight your vision, but if you persist and remain steadfast, you will definitely overcome them.

SPIRITUAL VISIONS

Spiritual visions can either be closed or open. They are wholly a means of communication between the spiritual realm and the physical realm. The source of the vision can be God or demonic influences.

Open Visions

These have to do with what we see with our spiritual eyes and hear with our spiritual ears.

Abraham had open visions as evidenced in Genesis 15:1:

> **"After these things the word of the LORD came unto Abram in a vision, saying, Fear not, Abram: I am thy shield, and thy exceeding great reward."**

Ezekiel had a similar experience in Ezekiel 1:1:

> **"as I was among the captives by the river of Chebar, that the heavens were opened, and I saw visions of God."**

Daniel in Daniel 8:2 also had open visions:

"And I saw in a vision; and it came to pass, when I saw, that I was at Shushan in the palace, which is in the province of Elam; and I saw in a vision, and I was by the river of Ulai."

In Acts 10:3, Cornelius

"saw in a vision evidently about the ninth hour of the day an angel of God coming in to him, and saying unto him, Cornelius."

Paul, in Acts 16:9 recounts,

"And a vision appeared to Paul in the night; There stood a man of Macedonia, and prayed him, saying, Come over into Macedonia, and help us."

Closed Visions

Open visions are so real and tangible to our physical senses that we feel as if we see them naturally with our eyes. Closed visions are also seen with the eyes of the Spirit but are not as tangible. They are barely perceptible, flashing before our mind's eye. However, they are very specific and straight to the point. They usually must be interpreted because they incorporate a great deal of symbolism.

One day while I was preaching, anytime I looked in the direction of a man seated in the front pew, I would see a coffin beside him. It happened about three times until I finally called him out to pray for him. The coffin represented the spirit of death. The vision was confirmed when the man revealed that the night before, both his wife and daughter had dreamt of him in a coffin! We prayed and rebuked the spirit of death hovering over his life.

I noticed that a visitor to my church seemed to be enveloped by darkness whenever I looked at her. We prayed against the spirit of witchcraft and it fled. It turned out that she was under the influence of witchcraft and demonic spirits. She later explained that she had often felt oppressed in her sleep by a force that weighed down on her. She had also heard voices in the night and something moving around her room when there was no one else there. These happenings came to a halt after she had been prayed for and became a committed Christian.

The gifts of the word of knowledge, the word of wisdom, and the discernment of the spirits can also operate through visions. The first example I gave was a word of knowledge given through a closed vision, while the second was the discernment of the spirits, which also came through a closed vision (see 1 Corinthians 12:8). Jesus Christ operated in this way as shown in Luke 10:18:

"And he said unto them, I beheld Satan as lightning fall from heaven."

Earlier, in my case studies on dreams, I referred to a woman in the ministry whom God had exposed as a witch. She finally

25

left the church as recounted following a vision that God gave my wife, Uzoamaka. This is her account:

"I was awake and suddenly I saw Pastor Uzor telling the congregation to kneel down and call unto God to expel every witch in the church. As we did so, with our hands pointing to heaven, the Spirit of the Lord told me to open my spiritual eyes. Suddenly, I saw that the woman was not pointing to heaven but to two other women nearby. Again, the Spirit of God told me to open my spiritual ears, and I realised that the woman's prayer was not in tune with ours. She was decreeing that the other women were witches and that they should die."

I knew that this was serious, and as God led me, I announced that I would expose the witch since revelations had kept coming about her. Less than a month later, the woman left the church without me even calling out her name.

Before I became a pastor, I had a vision of myself climbing the earth with multitudes following me. I did not know who they were, and I could not even turn back to see lest I fell. As I got to the top of the earth, I saw a small window, and I realised that I had to get through the window. It was so small that the slightest error of judgment would cause me to miss it. This window, I realised, was the window of heaven, and I stood in contemplation wondering how to get inside; then the vision ended. God then spoke to me clearly that He has called me to lead people to heaven.

As I said earlier, visions occur on a higher spiritual plain than dreams but have the same purpose. Both the biblical and personal examples I have shared show the importance and necessity of dreams and visions, especially in these end times. We need these revelations to direct, guide, inform, and protect us, to explain things to us, and also to expose the plans of the enemy. If we live in ignorance, despite our best efforts, we will always fall short of the perfect Will of God for our lives. We will never fulfil our destiny but merely exist in a state of hopelessness and despair. If God considers it vital, then I can assure you, dreams and visions should not be taken lightly; instead, they should be strongly desired.

Demonic Dreams and Visions

What are demonic dreams? They are dreams from the spiritual hosts of wickedness operating in the heavenlies. These should not be confused with the dreams that God gives to expose the plans and purposes of the kingdom of darkness. To clarify this difference, we need to go back to Ephesians 6:12:

> **"For we wrestle not against flesh and blood, but against principalities, against powers, against the rulers of the darkness of this world, against spiritual wickedness in high places."**

Satan and his demons can attach to someone in their dreams. He and his cohorts also appear as angels of light in dreams and visions to deceive people. This is confirmed in 2 Corinthians 11:14–15:

"And no marvel; for Satan himself is transformed into an angel of light. Therefore it is no great thing if his ministers also be transformed as the ministers of righteousness; whose end shall be according to their works."

So many people have been deceived and have deviated from God's revealed Word, forming doctrines of their own based on a so-called "angelic visitation." Most "Christian" cults and false religions originated from such encounters.

In my experience in counselling, women have told me how they have been forcefully and violently assaulted in their sleep by demonic beings or evil spirits in human form. After their ordeal, they are shocked to see what appears to be semen on their bodies. Clearly, these are satanic in origin. On the other hand, God may expose the kingdom of darkness through a dream or vision. Satan does not like his activities to be exposed, preferring to keep people deceived. An example of this is found in Ezekiel 8:6–17. Verse 12 reads:

"Then said he unto me, Son of man, hast thou seen what the ancients of the house of Israel do in the dark, every man in the chambers of his imagery? for they say, The LORD seeth us not; the LORD hath forsaken the earth."

In these last days, we should be extremely careful how we analyse our dreams and visions. They must be interpreted in the light of God's Word and under the direction of the Holy Spirit. Otherwise, we will be deceived, believing that all spiritual and supernatural experiences are from God. Divination, enchantments, and sorcery are some of the means that satanic agents use to bring about evil visions, and many people are deceived.

Even Christians sometimes patronise diviners and sorcerers in search of spiritual experiences and words for the future. This is why we must test every spirit:

> **"Beloved, believe not every spirit, but try the spirits whether they are of God: because many false prophets are gone out into the world"** (1 John 4:1).

Saul, a man anointed by God, reduced himself to the level of seeking supernatural knowledge from a witch:

> **"And when Saul enquired of the LORD, the LORD answered him not, neither by dreams, nor by Urim, nor by prophets. Then said Saul unto his servants, Seek me a woman that hath a familiar spirit, that I may go to her, and inquire of her. And his servants said to him, Behold, there is a woman that hath a familiar spirit at Endor"** (1 Samuel 28:6–7).

God condemned these practices, and we should heed that warning. See Leviticus 19:31:

> **"Regard not them that have familiar spirits, neither seek after wizards, to be defiled by them: I am the LORD your God."**

Compare this also with Jeremiah 14:14:

> **"Then the LORD said unto me, The prophets prophesy lies in my name: I sent them not, neither have I commanded them, neither spake unto them: they prophesy unto you a false vision and divination, and a thing of nought, and the deceit of their heart."**

Clearly, we should not seek spiritual knowledge and understanding of our dreams and visions outside the Word of God and the prompting of the Holy Spirit.

Chapter 3

Conditions for Dreams and Visions

What are the best conditions for receiving dreams and visions?

These are the conditions that activate or enhance revelations through dreams and visions. Suffice to say, God, who is sovereign, can and does speak to people without restrictions or reservations despite the absence of such conditions. However, as we will see, dreams and visions are much more prevalent under the following conditions:

The Night Atmosphere

What is so peculiar about the night atmosphere?

To understand the great significance of the night, we must

look at the beginning where it was first mentioned in the Bible to get a clear view and understanding of the word "night."

In Genesis 1:1–5, the Bible says:

"In the beginning God created the heaven and the earth. And the earth was without form, and void; and darkness was upon the face of the deep. And the Spirit of God moved upon the face of the waters. And God said, Let there be light: and there was light. And God saw the light, that it was good: and God divided the light from the darkness. And God called the light Day, and the darkness he called Night. And the evening and the morning were the first day."

There is so much that can be gleaned from the above passage of Scripture. Firstly, the name of darkness is Night (verse 5). Darkness came about consequently or as a by-product of creation. Scripture says that when God created heaven and earth, **"darkness was upon the face of the deep"** (verse 2). In other words, darkness was not something that God specifically created, it was a consequence of creation. God said: **"Let there be light and there was light"** (verse 3).

The order of creation shows that works of darkness, such as death, sickness, and misfortune, can come uninvited at any time; however, the positive works of light, such as long life, good health, and fortune, come only out of a conscious effort and the Grace of God upon our lives.

The deep in verse 2 implies things hidden beneath the surface. The word "deep" suggests a type of womb, which contains something and is waiting to give birth. It was out of the hidden womb of darkness that light was given birth to. It had been there all the time, but God's Word brought it forth and the Spirit of God hovering over the darkness brought it into manifestation. Since light originated from darkness, it follows that "night" is senior to "day." God refers to a 24-hour cycle as "evening and morning" so that a new day actually starts at 12 midnight (verse 5). This, therefore, helps to explain why revelations come forth more often in the womb of our night sleep than in the day. Light is synonymous with revelation and so when we are asleep at night, the Spirit of God is able to release the "light" of God's mind to us.

In view of this, the night is for spiritual action and the day is for the activity to be made manifest. In Job 33:14–18, we see clearly:

> **"For God speaketh once, yea twice, yet man perceiveth it not. In a dream, in a vision of the night, when deep sleep falleth upon men, in slumberings upon the bed; Then he openeth the ears of men, and sealeth their instruction, That he may withdraw man from his purpose, and hide pride from man. He keepeth back his soul from the pit, and his life from perishing by the sword."**

We see also in Genesis 32:24–26 that it was nighttime when Jacob wrestled with God, and he did not stop until it was daybreak:

> **"And Jacob was left alone; and there wrestled a man with him until the breaking of the day. And when he saw that he prevailed not against him, he touched the hollow of his thigh; and the hollow of Jacob's thigh was out of joint, as he wrestled with him. And he said, Let me go, for the day breaketh. And he said, I will not let thee go, except thou bless me."**

Wrestling here refers to prayer, and this passage reveals the importance of praying at night. Since the night is for creative purposes, when we pray at night, there is a greater tendency for us to have dreams and visions, bringing revelation about our circumstances.

In Genesis 1:3, God spoke and light (revelation) came out of the deep (darkness). In the same way, when we speak God's Word in prayer at night, revelations (light) through dreams and visions come forth. Jesus Christ, who is God and our example in life, prayed more at night. Luke 6:12 reads:

> **"And it came to pass in those days, that he went out into a mountain to pray, and continued all night in prayer to God."**

It was after this prayer that He received direction on whom to appoint as his twelve disciples. Jesus' prayers at night enabled Him to actualize His God-given destiny, particularly in His distress in the garden of Gethsemane (Matthew 26:36–43).

In moments of stress, it is quality time with the Lord at night that can keep you on top of your challenges. For it is at night that revelations concerning your situation are more likely to come:

> **"Rejoice not against me, O mine enemy: when I fall, I shall arise; when I sit in darkness, the LORD shall be a light unto me"** (Micah 7:8).

In my own and others' experiences, I have found this to be true. I always seem to be a step ahead of both my "enemies" and my contemporaries. That is the case in the ministry, and it was the same when I worked full-time in a bank. All the dreams and visions referred to earlier occurred at night after night prayers unto God. This helped me to become a success both in my former place of work and in my ministry.

When I was a bank manager, God would always reveal to me after praying at night when inspectors would come from the headquarters to audit my branch. Not only that, He would show me exactly who was coming and the specific areas they would be looking at. This gave me time to work on these areas, if necessary, and thus everything was always in order. I would always score above average and my overall performance was always an "A." This perplexed most of my colleagues. Even the headquarters' officials began to suspect that someone was giving me information about when the inspectors were coming since these visits were supposed to be a surprise. Without these revelations from God, there is no way that I could have obtained such consistent good reports.

It was also in the night that God showed me how another branch wanted to involve my branch in fraudulent activities. A very senior official was revealed to me as part of the conspiracy. God showed me what to do, and I escaped that conspiracy, which could have cost me my job. Many of my colleagues in positions of authority have lost their jobs because of fraud and conspiracies despite their innocence.

Many others have been held in bondage to poverty, curses, evil conspiracies, frustrations, failure, job loss, and marriage failure all because of either a lack of revelation or because they have forgotten or ignored their dreams and visions. Praying at night increases your capacity to receive revelation from God. The Bible says in Proverbs 20:13:

"Love not sleep, lest thou come to poverty; open thine eyes, and thou shalt be satisfied with bread."

Beloved, do not be deceived; what you do at night determines your future. Without weeping, wrestling, and striving at night through prayer, there will be no manifestation of what will bring you joy in the morning.

"Weeping may endure for a night, but joy cometh in the morning. And in my prosperity I said, I shall never be moved" (Psalm 30:5–6).

In ministry, this principle was no different. When I first began in ministry, I was very inexperienced and lacked any formal theological training. Since my entry into ministry happened quite suddenly, I decided to employ ministers who had formal theological qualifications. After praying at night, the Lord would show me my ministers discussing the issues they wanted to raise in our weekly meetings. It enabled me to prepare, and as we met, I applied wisdom to the sensitive issues they raised. Since God revealed things to me beforehand, I was always ready to diffuse their arguments. After a while, they began to suspect each other, accusing themselves of treachery. Little did they know that it was God exposing them. There is a similar event in the Bible in 2 Kings 6:8–12:

> **"Then the king of Syria warred against Israel, and took counsel with his servants, saying, In such and such a place shall be my camp. And the man of God sent unto the king of Israel, saying, Beware that thou pass not such a place; for thither the Syrians are come down. And the king of Israel sent to the place which the man of God told him and warned him of, and saved himself there, not once nor twice. Therefore the heart of the**

king of Syria was sore troubled for this thing; and he called his servants, and said unto them, Will ye not shew me which of us is for the king of Israel? And one of his servants said, None, my lord, O king: but Elisha, the prophet that is in Israel, telleth the king of Israel the words that thou speakest in thy bedchamber."

Most crises in churches — the Body of Christ — could have been averted if the right atmosphere had been taken advantage of. How many churches have closed down today by reason of a lack of revelation from God exposing the conspiracies of the enemy? Because Christians do not seek clear directives from God concerning the course a ministry should take, many pastors have begun to look to the world and apply all sorts of worldly and human wisdom in running their ministries.

In John 2:16, Jesus said

"unto them that sold doves, Take these things hence; make not my Father's house an house of merchandise."

In Luke 19:46, He also says:

"It is written, My house is the house of prayer: but ye have made it a den of thieves."

For some churches, prayer is no longer key. Instead, the emphasis is on monetary gain with pastors packaging it as being the Lord's work. One of the effective ways to stop the gates of hell from prevailing (Matthew 16:18) is through serious intercession both at night and during the day. 1 Thessalonians 5:17 encourages us to **"pray without ceasing."**

When I set up my first church, Jesus Sanctuary Ministries in Nigeria, there were many attacks, both physical and spiritual. The church was in a Government Reserve Area, Onitsha, which is mainly residential. However, God showed me in a dream that that was where the church should be. This revelation was later confirmed by others. There had never been a church in the centre of the area before, but I went ahead on God's Word and built the church there. I was later sued, but in the end, God gave us the victory. Left to myself, I would have had a hall in town, but once God revealed His Will, I obeyed and the church is all the better for it. Without those revelations, I would have made a mistake that would have affected the ministry.

Unfortunately, satanic forces, occultists, and agents of darkness have a greater understanding of the strength of the night than the average Christian who should be using it to their advantage. Evil conspiracies and gatherings often occur under the cover of the night. Enchantments, divinations, spells, and incantations are practised at night with the manifestations of such evil in the daytime. Proverbs 4:16–17 says:

"For they sleep not, except they have done mischief; and their sleep is taken away,

unless they cause some to fall. For they eat the bread of wickedness, and drink the wine of violence."

Those who rally against you do not sleep. They are active at night and bring forth evil. To counteract this, you must also take advantage of the night atmosphere by praying at night. It was at night that Judas led the chief priests and elders to arrest Jesus in the Garden of Gethsemane (Matthew 26:47). He was also judged at night (Matthew 26:59–66) and then crucified during the day. In the parable of the wheat and tares in Matthew 13:24–30, it was at night that the enemy came — see verse 25:

"But while men slept, his enemy came and sowed tares among the wheat, and went his way."

It was not only at night that the enemy came but when the men were asleep. If the men were awake, it would have been impossible for the enemy to come. When we give ourselves to praying at night, it will be difficult for the enemy to perform their evil deeds.

Fasting and Prayer

Fasting means abstaining from food and liquids for a certain period to separate oneself unto God to seek His face in concentrated prayer. Fasting kills the flesh and its attendant desires and causes your spirit to be more sensitive and receptive to the things of the Spirit.

Another word for the operation of the flesh is carnality. In Romans 8:5–8, the Bible says:

> **"For they that are after the flesh do mind the things of the flesh; but they that are after the Spirit the things of the Spirit. For to be carnally minded is death; but to be spiritually minded is life and peace. Because the carnal mind is enmity against God: for it is not subject to the law of God, neither indeed can be. So then they that are in the flesh cannot please God."**

The carnal mind is not renewed by the Word of God (Romans 12:1–2) but possesses the same nature as one who is not born again. Carnality is manifested in what the Bible refers to as the works of the flesh. Galatians 5:19–21 says:

> **"Now the works of the flesh are manifest, which are these; Adultery, fornication, uncleanness, lasciviousness, Idolatry, witchcraft, hatred, variance, emulations, wrath, strife, seditions, heresies, Envyings, murders, drunkenness, revellings, and such like: of the which I tell you before, as I have also told you in time past, that they which do such things shall not inherit the kingdom of God."**

These Scriptures show clearly that the flesh is the strongest enemy of the spirit of mankind. Conversely, fasting and prayer is the number one enemy of the flesh. The flesh and the spirit are opposed to each other. You cannot be in the flesh and walk in God's Will or receive revelation from God, neither can you be in the spirit and manifest the works of the flesh. That is why even when God reveals things to sinners, it is usually when they are fast asleep.

"This I say then, Walk in the Spirit, and ye shall not fulfil the lust of the flesh. For the flesh lusteth against the Spirit, and the Spirit against the flesh: and these are contrary the one to the other: so that ye cannot do the things that ye would" (Galatians 5:16–17).

Jesus did not start His public ministry until he had been through a period of fasting and prayer (Matthew 4:1–17 and Luke 4:1–15). After He came out of the wilderness, Luke 4:14 recounts:

"And Jesus returned in the power of the Spirit into Galilee: and there went out a fame of him through all the region round about."

This led to the manifestations of the gifts of the Spirit, including the gifts of revelation. He could pick the right apostles as a result.

It was also during a time of prayer that Cornelius, the Roman Centurion, received a vision from God:

> **"There was a certain man in Caesarea called Cornelius, a centurion of the band called the Italian band, A devout man, and one that feared God with all his house, which gave much alms to the people, and prayed to God alway. He saw in a vision evidently about the ninth hour of the day an angel of God coming in to him, and saying unto him, Cornelius"** (Acts 10:1–3).

The same is also seen with Peter in Acts 10:9–10:

> **"On the morrow, as they went on their journey, and drew nigh unto the city, Peter went up upon the housetop to pray about the sixth hour: And he became very hungry, and would have eaten: but while they made ready, he fell into a trance."**

Ezekiel, Isaiah, Daniel, Paul, and other prophets and apostles lived a life of fasting and prayer and, as a result, operated mightily in the supernatural with many revelations from God. In contemporary times, Martin Luther, John Calvin, Charles Finney, Charles Haddon Spurgeon, John Wesley, Smith Wigglesworth, Maria Woodworth-Etter, and Katherine Kuhlman were men and women of prayer and fasting. The revelations they received helped them to overcome the obstacles in their spiritual journeys.

Great Men of God today such as Benny Hinn, Pastor E.A. Adeboye, and Reverend Ezekiel of the Christian Pentecostal Mission would not have had the spiritual impact they have today without fasting and prayer.

Scripture reveals that some people's spiritual eyes and ears are blind and deaf respectively to God (Matthew 13:14–15). Fasting and prayer can cause the spirit-man of a person to come alive and to be more receptive to the things of the Spirit. Our "spiritual antenna" (spiritual eyes and ears) become attuned to receive messages in the spiritual realm that come through revelation.

In these turbulent times, I cannot understand how some Christians see fasting and prayer as outdated and unnecessary for their spiritual growth. They denounce it as "spiritual legalism." Unfortunately, this is a belief propagated by Satan, the father of all lies (John 8:44). Consequently, most Christians today are both spiritually blind and deaf, as Jeremiah put it in Jeremiah 5:21:

"Hear now this, O foolish people, and without understanding; which have eyes, and see not; which have ears, and hear not."

Man's spiritual eyes and ears become closed because of sin. When Adam and Eve were sinless, their spiritual eyes and ears were open and their understanding was perfect. Sin, however, brought an end to this. The flesh took control and their physical eyes and ears took precedence over their spiritual senses. If we fail to develop our spiritual perception through fasting and prayer, the consequences will be very serious. We have only to look at the church today, which downplays fasting and prayer. It has become dead without fire or direction. Preachers and ministries rely on "methodologies" because no one is willing to pay the price of fasting and prayer. The church is a spiritual body and cannot be run using carnal means or human ideas and wisdom. We need to seek revelation from God to keep us on the right track.

If we throw fasting and prayer to the winds, what do we expect to see in our lives and ministries? The church has become like **"clouds… without water"** (Jude 1:12), **"Having a form of godliness, but denying the power thereof"** (2 Timothy 3:5).

Unless we seek revelation, we will not be aware of the wiles of the enemy against the church. We will, therefore, be unable to penetrate the strongholds and spirits of the land that hold the people in bondage. Even when we lift half-hearted prayers, they will be like misdirected arrows because we are unaware of the operations of the kingdom of darkness.

Although there is an increase in spiritual knowledge and its dissemination via visual and written media, there is no lasting impact on the world with little fruit to show for it. Without fasting and prayer, there is no outpouring of the Spirit (Acts 1:4, 8, 13–14; 2:1–4, 17–18). Verses 17 and 18 of Acts 2 correspond with Joel 2:28–29. The outpouring of the

Spirit brought vision. In Joel 2:15, a fast was called after which we see an abundance of the former and latter rain in verses 19, 23–29. This refers to the outpouring of the Holy Spirit and the resultant effects.

In 2 Chronicles 20:2–3, Jehoshaphat called a fast when the children of Moab, Ammon, and others gathered against Israel. In verse 14, the Spirit of God appeared and an instruction was given on how to overcome these enemies. Without the revelation, they would have gone into battle and failed woefully. As instructed by God, they simply praised and worshipped God, and their enemies were defeated. How many churches would have prevailed against satanic attacks, within and without, if only they had given themselves to fasting and prayer? Human solutions are not the answer to spiritual problems. Only God can provide the answers that we need. We do not see as He sees or understand as He does (Isaiah 55:8–9).

At Jesus Sanctuary, we start the year with fasting and prayer, sometimes for 40 or 50 days and nights. Also, the first two days of every month are set aside for fasting and prayer and many revelations have come forth. This gives us direction as to what we are to do for the year, the prospects and the problems we are going to encounter. Individual church members also receive revelations about their lives and families, and it provides a kind of spiritual timetable.

Testimony One: It was during a period of fasting and prayer that God revealed who would take over as the pastor for the branch of the ministry at Onitsha. I already had someone in mind, but God showed me someone else. Had it not been for God's revelation, it would not even have crossed my mind to appoint him.

Testimony Two: It was also during a season of fasting and prayer that a worker in the church was exposed as having ties to the occult. He had left the occult and openly condemned those involved in it, having testified against them. However, it was revealed that he was still holding on to things of the occult and pretending to me and everyone else that he was not.

Testimony Three: A lady in the church who had been trying for years to have a baby received her solution during fasting and prayer. Apparently, occultists had spiritually chained her womb with a padlock and key. God destroyed the chain and padlock, and less than two months later, she was pregnant and is now a proud mother.

Testimony Four: During fasting and prayer, a man with a serious, debilitating pain in his leg received a revelation on the cause of his pain. He saw something like a snake coming out of his leg, and in the revelation, he killed it. That was the end of the leg pain. Had it not been for the revelation, he would have assumed it was normal because he is about seventy years of age.

Most problems and illnesses that Christians experience have spiritual causes. We should not assume that all physical problems are simply a sign of the natural ageing of the body. After all, Moses died at 120 years and **"his eye was not dim, nor his natural force abated"** (Deuteronomy 34:7).

Holiness and Righteousness

Holiness and righteousness are in direct opposition to sinfulness and unrighteousness. Just as sin and unrighteousness separate us from God (Isaiah 59:2), holiness and righteousness keep us in His Presence and keep the "spiritual communication lines" open to revelation from God. The Bible makes it clear in Hebrews 12:14:

> **"Follow peace with all men, and holiness, without which no man shall see the Lord."**

We also see Jesus in Matthew 5:8 declaring,

> **"Blessed are the pure in heart: for they shall see God."**

In Psalm 24:3–4, it is echoed,

> **"Who shall ascend into the hill of the LORD? or who shall stand in his holy place? He that hath clean hands, and a pure heart; who hath not lifted up his soul unto vanity, nor sworn deceitfully."**

Purity is synonymous with holiness and righteousness, and the Scriptures above show that this greatly increases our ability to receive revelations from God. Those who received revelations through trances and out-of-body experiences in the Bible lived lives of holiness and righteousness. We cannot come face-to-face with God without holiness and righteousness (Exodus 33:17–23 and Exodus 34:29–35). If we desire to move into a higher realm of revelation, we need to make holiness our goal. In 1 Peter 1:15–16, Peter wrote:

"But as he which hath called you is holy, so be ye holy in all manner of conversation; Because it is written, Be ye holy; for I am holy."

Ezekiel also operated in this realm. Ezekiel 8:3 reads:

"And he put forth the form of an hand, and took me by a lock of mine head; and the spirit lifted me up between the earth and the heaven, and brought me in the visions of God to Jerusalem, to the door."

I have found this to be true in my own life. When I was made a pastor, I was inexperienced, inadequate, and generally lacked "spiritual know-how." But I openly made a vow to God in relation to holiness and righteousness that I would never defile myself sexually or otherwise and asked the church to pray for me. I asked God in return to bless the ministry and manifest His Spirit and Power through me.

Believe it or not, some elders came to advise me that I had placed the altar "too high" and would not be able to achieve and maintain the standard. They even quoted

Scriptures to prove their argument. The point I want to make here is that after the vow, there was a mighty increase in revelation. Within four years, the church had grown phenomenally both spiritually and numerically and had a great deal of influence. The crises that came to the church, both within and without, were all revealed. We prayed and the crises were averted and problems solved without any shaking or noticeable problem to the church.

We became a source of scandal. Other churches published magazines accusing us of operating in occult power and using familiar spirits because of the level of revelation in which we operated. They could not see how else the signs and wonders in our church came about. They wondered how this inexperienced former banker could achieve in two years what they had been unable to achieve in over ten or fifteen years.

Despite this, the ministry began to grow in leaps and bounds. Every Judas and potential troublemaker was exposed through revelation even before they began to make their moves. What would have destroyed other ministries instead kept us strong and growing, much to the surprise of the agents of darkness both within and without the Body of Christ.

Holiness and righteousness should be everyone's heart's desire. If we want to speak to God face-to-face and receive revelations and prophecies, holiness and righteousness should be our watchwords. We are the Temple of God (1 Corinthians 3:17) and are to keep the Temple holy. Otherwise, God will depart. Holiness brings us into closer intimacy with God and, as a result, nothing will be hidden from us by God, unless He does not want us to know.

Today, trances and out-of-body experiences are rare because the church has adopted the standard of the world. People living holy and righteous lives are looked at as outdated, outmoded, living in the dark ages, or "holier-than-thou." Since when did the standards of God become outdated? We are the light, not the wind, and we should not take our example from the world. James 4:4 says:

> **"Ye adulterers and adulteresses, know ye not that the friendship of the world is enmity with God? whosoever therefore will be a friend of the world is the enemy of God."**

Paul in 2 Corinthians 6:14–17 says:

> **"Be ye not unequally yoked together with unbelievers: for what fellowship hath righteousness with unrighteousness? and what communion hath light with darkness? And what concord hath Christ with Belial? or what part hath he that believeth with an infidel? And what agreement hath the temple of God with idols? for ye are the temple of the living God; as God hath said, I will dwell in them, and walk in them; and I will be their God, and they shall be my**

people. Wherefore come out from among them, and be ye separate, saith the Lord, and touch not the unclean thing; and I will receive you."

Surprisingly, this principle of holiness and righteousness is true even in the kingdom of darkness. A native doctor confessed after his conversion to Christianity how he had to separate himself from everything immoral, unclean, and sinful for two weeks before the demonic marine spirit would agree to appear before him. In Africa, the native doctors, occultists, evil priests, and priestesses abstain from sexual contact with their spouses when they want revelations from the spirit world. They sever contact with anyone they feel will cause uncleanliness in their lives so they can remain "pure and separated" unto the kingdom of darkness. If this is so for the agents of darkness, how much more does it apply to us as the children of God?

Chapter 4

Killers and Promoters of Dreams and Visions

A woman dreamed that she saw her three children burning in a fire. She woke up perplexed and told her husband, fearing for the lives of her children. They were still at boarding school and yet to come home for the vacation. Her husband brushed her fears aside, believing that she was being unnecessarily anxious. About a week or so after, their children left school and the woman and her husband went to pick them up at the airport. Right before their eyes, the plane crash-landed and burst into flames, killing her children and the other passengers.

When we have such revelations, it is a warning for us to pray and take the necessary precautionary measures; we must therefore not push them aside. I have come across many similar instances such as this in the Bible, but there was one that struck me greatly in my formative years as a

Christian. This is the story of the plot by Herod to kill Jesus. Many, including myself, would reason that God could have destroyed Herod. Instead, He chose to reveal Herod's plot with careful instructions to Joseph:

"And when they were departed, behold, the angel of the Lord appeareth to Joseph in a dream, saying, Arise, and take the young child and his mother, and flee into Egypt, and be thou there until I bring thee word: for Herod will seek the young child to destroy him" (Matthew 2:13).

I have asked myself this question severally: What if Joseph had disregarded the dream and God's instructions on the basis that since Jesus was the prophesied Messiah and Son of God, nothing would happen to Him? What then would have been the fate of our Lord and Saviour Jesus Christ?

God's ways and thoughts are not like ours and so it lies with us to be careful to take His revelations and instructions to us seriously. We are not to take anything for granted, for God alone chooses the way He will intervene in a matter. How many tragic events and wrong choices could have been avoided in our lives if only we took the time to heed God's revelations to us? We must be mindful of certain factors for the success or failure of the revelations God gives us, whether they are to warn us, to expose something, to reveal God's plan of blessing us, to promote us and our gifts to men, or even a puzzle needing to be solved.

Some revelations are to be cancelled through prayer, whilst others are to be decoded, all with the help and guidance of the Holy Spirit and the Word of God. In Exodus 32:10–11 & 14, God appeared to Moses and told him that He would destroy Israel. Moses interceded, and the plan God had was cancelled:

> **"Now therefore let me alone, that my wrath may wax hot against them, and that I may consume them: and I will make of thee a great nation. And Moses besought the LORD his God, and said, LORD, why doth thy wrath wax hot against thy people, which thou hast brought forth out of the land of Egypt with great power, and with a mighty hand. And the LORD repented of the evil which he thought to do unto his people."**

When it comes to claiming things for ourselves as Christians, the Bible makes us understand that:

> **"Thou shalt also decree a thing, and it shall be established unto thee"** (Job 22:28).

Revelations in Genesis 41 and Daniel 4 & 5 were puzzles to be decoded by an Anointed Servant of God.

Manifestations of the Flesh

One of the factors that can affect the success or failure of a revelation is the manifestation of the flesh.

Impatience

One way it manifests itself is through impatience. As earlier indicated, Abraham, for example, had waited so long for God's promise of a son to materialise that he promptly agreed to his wife's suggestion and slept with Hagar (Genesis 16:1–4), who conceived and gave birth to Ishmael. He was not the promised child, and his birth is the cause of the problems we face in the Middle East today:

> **"And he will be a wild man; his hand will be against every man, and every man's hand against him"** (Genesis 16:12).

Moses knew that he was called to deliver his people but impatience caused him to act before time. Exodus 2:11–12, 15 reads:

> **"and he spied an Egyptian smiting an Hebrew, one of his brethren. And he looked this way and that way... he slew the Egyptian, and hid him in the sand... he sought to slay Moses. But Moses fled from the face of Pharaoh, and dwelt in the land of Midian."**

As a result of impatience, I went ahead of God's timing to pray for the dead to be raised to life after receiving a revelation that I would be used in this way.

Sin

Another manifestation of the flesh is sin. God had given the land of Canaan to the Israelites, promising them victory every step of the way. After the fall of Jericho, the next battle with Ai saw the Israelites defeated (Joshua 7:4–5). The reason being that Achan sinned and disobeyed the commandment of God (Joshua 7:21). Sin in our lives can result in unforeseen consequences that may hinder or slow down the manifestation of God's revelations to us.

Presumption

When God called Abraham out, He did not instruct him to go with Lot (Genesis 12:4). It was thus not until Lot separated from Abraham that God showed him the land he had given to him (Genesis 134:14–18). We must follow God's exact instructions for our revelations to come to pass and not delay or be destroyed.

Fear and Doubt

Fear and doubt can also affect how a revelation manifests in the natural. God promised the Israelites the promised land but when the spies Moses had sent out came back, they were full of discouraging words. Instead of holding on to God's Word, they allowed fear and doubt to grip their hearts and control them (Numbers 13:25–33). Verse 31 reads:

"But the men that went up with him said, We be not able to go up against the people; for they are stronger than we."

This caused the Israelites to rebel, and they could not fulfil the destiny that had been promised them (Numbers 14:1–32).

Satan

Satan seeks also to affect our revelations. He comes to kill, steal, and destroy (John 10:10) and will do his best to destroy that which God has promised and revealed. In Matthew 2, Herod tried to kill Jesus and destroy His destiny. The realm of the Spirit is open and you can receive revelations not only about yourself but also about others. After all, both the wise men and the shepherds out in the fields received revelations about Jesus' birth (Matthew 2:9–10 and Luke 2:8–14), as did Mary (Luke 1:26–35) and Joseph (Matthew 1:18–25). We need to wage active warfare against Satan (Ephesians 6:12–18) and be sensitive to his wiles and deceptive ways (Genesis 3:1–8).

Friends

Friends can encourage or destroy your dreams and visions. In 1 Kings 12:1–19, Rehoboam, Solomon's son, reigned in his stead. The elders advised him on how to rule in order to win the people's heart.

> **"Thy father made our yoke grievous: now therefore make thou the grievous service of thy father, and his heavy yoke which he put upon us, lighter, and we will serve thee. And they spake unto him, saying, If thou wilt be a servant unto this people this day, and wilt serve them, and answer them, and speak good words to them, then they will be thy servants for ever. But he forsook the counsel of the old men"** (verses 4, 7–8).

Instead, Rehoboam took the counsel of his friends and age mates.

> **"thus shalt thou say unto them, My little finger shall be thicker than my father's loins. And now whereas my father did lade you with a heavy yoke, I will add to your yoke: my father hath chastised you with whips, but I will chastise you with scorpions"** (verses 10–11).

The result was that Israel no longer remained one and separated into the kingdom of Israel and the kingdom of Judah.

> **"So when all Israel saw that the king hearkened not unto them, the people answered the king, saying, What portion have we in David? neither have we inheritance in the son of Jesse: to your tents, O Israel: now see to thine own house, David. So Israel departed unto their tents"**
> (1 Kings 12:16).

When I wanted to start my television ministry around 1999, some men of God advised against it. They said that the TV ministry was double-edged, meaning it could either build or destroy a ministry and hence, I would be wise not to take that risk. I ignored them and followed God's leading. Today, the television ministry has spread to places I never envisaged possible. People from all over Nigeria recognise me and the ministry wherever that I go, and the television exposure has led to a phenomenal growth in the ministry. Be careful therefore who you relate your dream or vision to, for they can make or break you. There were also men and women of God who encouraged me greatly in the television ministry, and I thank God for them.

Job's friends almost derailed him if not for his faith and trust in God (Job 4–36). Even if we do not have encouragers around us, we should hold fast to God's Word and His revelation to us despite the apparently conflicting circumstances and, like David, encourage ourselves in the Lord. 1 Samuel 30:6 reads:

"And David was greatly distressed... but David encouraged himself in the LORD his God."

Family

Members of our family can also affect our revelations positively or negatively. Joseph's brothers tried to kill his dream by selling him off as a slave to the Ishmaelites (Genesis 37:27–28). Do not think that the members of your family will accept or recognise what God wants to use you for. They may very well be the stumbling blocks to the achievement of your dream. David's father and brothers did not share in Samuel's proclamation that he was chosen by God to be king over Israel; his father did not even consider calling him at first (1 Samuel 16:5–11). In 1 Samuel 17:28, Eliab, David's brother, responded to him in a manner that demonstrated how much he despised him. He refused to acknowledge that David was anointed king and he tried to belittle him by suggesting that he go back and look after his sheep.

Samson's wife, Delilah, was the instrument used by the enemy to destroy Samson's destiny (Judges 16:4–21). Even Jesus' family almost derailed him; they did not do it out of jealousy but out of human concern. Sometimes, because of fear and concern, our family can become overprotective and misunderstand our calling (Matthew 12:46–50). Hannah in the Old Testament is also a good example. She was barren and being provoked by her adversary, Penninah. Elkanah tried to console her in 1 Samuel 1:8:

"Then said Elkanah her husband to her, Hannah, why weepest thou? and why eatest thou not? and why is thy heart grieved? am not I better to thee than ten sons?"

Should she have been satisfied with his sympathy, she would not have gone ahead to seek the Lord for a child who became one of the greatest prophets that ever lived (1 Samuel 1:1–19).

We need to align ourselves with God's Word or revelation. For God to reveal something to us is one thing but for us to agree with it is another. It is our agreement that brings the dream into manifestation. Mary agreed with God's Word given to her through the vision of the angel Gabriel:

"And, behold, thou shalt conceive in thy womb, and bring forth a son, and shalt call his name JESUS. He shall be great, and shall be called the Son of the Highest: and the Lord God shall give unto him the throne of his father David: And the angel answered and said unto her, The Holy Ghost shall come upon thee, and the power of the Highest shall overshadow thee: therefore also that

holy thing which shall be born of thee shall be called the Son of God. And Mary said, Behold the handmaid of the Lord; be it unto me according to thy word. And the angel departed from her" (Luke 1:31–38).

We should not allow the delayed manifestation of our dreams to cause us to doubt and lose faith. The Bible enjoins us to

"hold fast the profession of our faith without wavering; (for he is faithful that promised;)" (Hebrews 10:23).

The Word of God says in Amos 3:3,

"Can two walk together, except they be agreed?"

We must agree with our revelations and continue to confess that agreement and it shall come to pass. On the other hand, if the revelations are negative, we must pray and cancel them out. If we do not, the negative revelations will come to pass.

Chapter 5

Important Tips on Good Dreams and Visions

In 2005, on the last day of the church's fifty days and nights fasting and prayer, I remember vividly a dialogue I had with the Lord. As usual, during the fasting period, many revelations came forth, both good and bad, but I was concerned that the good revelations would take some time to come into manifestation, unlike the bad ones.

The Lord told me that most people, including myself, tend to give immediate attention to bad revelations by praying seriously against their manifestation. With the good revelations, however, we note them down and just sit back waiting for their manifestation after the initial excitement of their revelation. This is not right — the good revelations need to be given as much attention as the bad ones.

We must be careful to note that the fact that a revelation comes from God does not mean it cannot be hindered. A good example of this can be seen in Daniel 10:12–13 where the prince of Persia resisted the answer to Daniel's prayer:

> **"Then said he unto me, Fear not, Daniel: for from the first day that thou didst set thine heart to understand, and to chasten thyself before thy God, thy words were heard, and I am come for thy words. But the prince of the kingdom of Persia withstood me one and twenty days: but, lo, Michael, one of the chief princes, came to help me; and I remained there with the kings of Persia."**

God had promised that He would turn around the captivity of the Israelites after 70 years. This time frame had passed and yet they were still in bondage. Daniel discovered this promise and committed himself to prayer for its manifestation (Daniel 9:2–19). This is where Satan's demon, the prince of Persia, blocked the answer to his prayers. This goes to show that God's promise or revelation must be prayed through, otherwise, there will be no manifestation. Also, the prayers must continue until the manifestation is seen because the answer can be hindered. As the Word of God confirms in Matthew 18:18:

> **"Whatsoever ye shall bind on earth shall be bound in heaven: and whatsoever ye shall loose on earth shall be loosed in heaven."**

Not only are we required to bind the enemy, we are to loose the Word and Promise of God for our lives in order to bring them into manifestation.

The following Scriptures and prayers will aid you in the manifestation of your good revelations:

- Romans 6:23 — I confess my sins and declare that Jesus is Lord over my life and my personal saviour.

- 1 Thessalonians 5:18 — God, I thank You for my life and Your mercies towards me and all that concerns me.

- Joel 2:28 — I thank You God for pouring out Your Spirit upon me and opening my spiritual eyes for direction through Your revelation to the fulfilment of my dream and vision in Jesus' Name.

- Genesis 21:1 — I thank You God and decree that my good dreams and visions will come into manifestation today in Jesus' Name.

- Habakkuk 2:2–3 — I thank You God that none of my good revelations will be delayed in the spiritual realm in Jesus' Name.

- Genesis 37:28 — O Lord, I thank You that no power or authority will be able to destroy my good revelations in Jesus' Name.

- Daniel 10:12–13 and Matthew 18:18 — Every demonic power in the realm of the spirit withstanding the manifestation of my good revelations, I bind you now and command you to lose your hold over the manifestation of my revelations in Jesus' Name!

Chapter 6

Interpretations of Dreams and Visions

It is one thing to dream or receive visions and it is another to interpret them. This is because revelations come from the realm of the spirit and therefore we cannot use human understanding to interpret them or else we will commit a gross mistake. We need to seek God and His Word to determine exactly what we have seen and how we are to respond to it. In Genesis 41, Pharaoh sought the interpretation of his dream and by the Anointing and Gift of the Holy Spirit, Joseph not only interpreted the dream but also gave a solution for it.

I will go ahead now to share with you some real-life interpretations to deepen your understanding.

Interpretation One: In 1994, about a year after I had become a branch manager, I dreamed that I was driving over a bridge, steering with one hand and trying to catch a fish on a hook with the other. The fish was very large and I had to concentrate as I held it and not allow it to slip from my grip. As a result, I failed to see a big truck coming at me at top speed. By the time I took notice of it, it was almost upon me. I put my head down and the truck passed over me without harming me in any way. I stood up and immediately caught the fish. I prayed to God and He revealed the meaning of the dream. Notice that there were two symbols — the fish and the big truck. Catching fish in a dream generally speaks of wealth or financial blessings. Luke 5:4 & 6 and Matthew 17:27 read respectively:

> **"Now when he had left speaking, he said unto Simon, Launch out into the deep, and let down your nets for a draught. And when they had this done, they inclosed a great multitude of fishes: and their net brake."**

> **"Notwithstanding, lest we should offend them, go thou to the sea, and cast an hook, and take up the fish that first cometh up; and when thou hast opened his mouth, thou shalt find a piece of money."**

The truck moving at top speed is more obvious as its aim was to destroy or kill its target. The interpretation, therefore, was that I was in a position to make a lot of money for the bank, but an attack was being conspired against me to destroy me and thereby cut me off from my source of income. Shortly after the dream, a fraud was discovered in another branch of the bank, which my branch would have been dragged into. It would most likely have cost me my job and career and of course my source of income. Just like the truck in the dream, the fraud did not affect my branch. Instead, my branch was commended for its performance and diligence.

Interpretation Two: In another dream I had in 2001, I saw myself on a long wooden platform divided into three sections. As I moved through the three sections to the outside, I saw a magnificent house made of pure gold to which I was strongly attracted. Its roof was made of gold and white diamonds and the walls and gate surrounding it were of pure gold as well. I stepped down from the platform and approached the house. Suddenly, I saw a huge dog that was the same colour as the house, standing guard. As soon as I got close, the dog barked at me, and I ran back to the platform. God used my wife and a pastor friend who have the gift of interpretation of dreams to convey its meaning to me.

The wooden platform represented the ministry I was in at that time, while the golden house depicted the ministry God had given to me. The dog symbolised the "household enemy" (Matthew 10:36) sent against me, which is a type of Saul (spirit of opposition). Because the dog was the same colour as the house, it appeared to be a part of the ministry but it rather stood for strong opposition to my ministry. I needed faith and courage to leave where I was to get to where God had ordained me to be. The barking of the dog symbolised the negative predictions of those who considered themselves to be spiritually informed. I did not allow these predictions to cause me to lose courage and retreat; I persevered and established the ministry God has blessed me with today.

There are some symbols here worth looking at before I explain how the dream came to pass. The colour white denotes purity, while wood represents work in the household of God that has no eternal value. 1 Corinthians 3:12–13 & 15 reads:

"Now if any man build upon this foundation gold, silver, precious stones, wood, hay, stubble; Every man's work shall be made manifest: for the day shall declare it, because it shall be revealed by fire; and the fire shall try every man's work of what sort it is. If any man's work shall be burned, he shall suffer loss: but he himself shall be saved; yet so as by fire."

From the Scripture above, we can also glean that gold signifies a work of eternal value. It also represents a vessel unto honour and priesthood. 2 Timothy 2:20 declares:

"But in a great house there are not only vessels of gold and of silver, but also of

wood and of earth; and some to honour, and
some to dishonour."

The dog in gold, as I mentioned earlier, appeared to be a
vessel unto honour and a part of my ministry, but in reality,
was a household enemy. In the Bible, dogs have a negative
connotation, as illustrated in Matthew 7:6, Philippians 3:2,
and Revelation 22:15, respectively:

"Give not that which is holy unto the dogs...
lest they trample them under their feet, and
turn again and rend you."

"Beware of dogs, beware of evil workers,
beware of the concision."

"For without are dogs, and sorcerers, and
whoremongers, and murderers, and
idolaters, and whosoever loveth and maketh
a lie."

Following this dream and many others, I left the ministry I
was involved in to start my own. A trusted friend, confidant,
and minister who was a source of encouragement and help
turned against me and tried to hinder and destroy the
ministry, but because I was already praying, everything blew
over and he left the ministry.

When it comes to interpretation, there are certain
considerations to be taken into account. For the gift of
interpretation to be effective, the gift of discernment must

also operate. A sound knowledge of the Word of God is also necessary, for God does not say anything contrary to His Word. Discernment is not suspicion or strong personal feelings of right or wrong but a spiritual gift given by God to enable the perception of the spirit behind something and to rightly denote that which is good and that which is evil.

Not all symbols mean the same thing in every dream as the context of the dream must also be taken into consideration. For example, I dreamed that a lion was looking for me to attack me; I was above it and it could not find me. Here, the lion is Satan seeking destruction. 1 Peter 5:8 reads:

> **"Be sober, be vigilant; because your adversary the devil, as a roaring lion, walketh about, seeking whom he may devour."**

Conversely, Jesus is referred to as "the Lion of the tribe of Juda" (Revelation 5:5) so discernment and knowledge of the Word of God are vital or the wrong interpretation will be given, which could result in grave consequences. I will give some examples.

Example One: In 1999, I was still working full-time as a bank manager. I dreamed that one of my hands was more than double its size and it was shaking. Then I heard a voice say that my hand was in danger. I woke up frightened and confused and decided to consult my pastor. He told me that the dream was demonic and that I was under satanic attack and needed deliverance prayers. I had no peace in my spirit but since I knew no better, I did not argue and went back to work. A well-known evangelist who was a close family friend came to do some business in the bank and I decided to share the dream with her. She promised to seek God for the revelation and let me know what He said. She later told me that God said He had given me healing and deliverance power and that one of the ways it would operate would be through that particular hand. Also, anything I blessed with that hand would be blessed and anyone whom I prayed for would receive an answer. About three years after the dream, I began to see the manifestation of this revelation. If I had listened to my pastor, the story would definitely have been different.

Example Two: My wife also had a dream that was wrongly interpreted. In that dream, she saw herself walking down a wide, newly graded road. At the end of the road, she saw a construction company moulding a huge white cross that had to be held by a crane. She offered to help and they agreed and told her to carry the cross up a flight of several steps to a church at the top. As she stood wondering how she could achieve what a large crane could not, the crane dropped the cross on her head. To her great surprise, it was light and easy for her to carry. She was confronted with forces of opposition on her way up but none could defeat her. Instead, the cross kept knocking them out of her way and destroying them. As she reached the top of the steps, a large hand from heaven came down, lifted the cross from her head, and mounted it on the roof of the church. Inside the church, she saw her father, his sisters, and her own siblings with some other people. A Man of God was preaching that the Church of God needed the light and power of God because everywhere was dimly lit. The pastor to whom she related the dream said that her father was about to die thus the reason for which she was carrying a cross; she, therefore, had to pray. This interpretation was completely wrong. My wife took it upon herself and sought the face of God for which He revealed to her that He had placed a calling and a burden upon her life for souls. If she had listened to the pastor, she would never have known God's mind.

Sometimes, a dream or vision can elicit envy and jealousy from others. Due to these negative emotions, the person to whom we relate our dreams and visions can deliberately give us the wrong interpretation to keep us from the right path. Truth be told, some people may simply not have the gifts of discernment and interpretation.

Another factor to bear in mind with regards to interpretation is our natural perception or understanding of things. We should never allow natural, physical, or carnal things or events to cloud our spiritual judgment of a matter. Undoubtedly, God who is sovereign can use a perception in the natural for the interpretation of revelation at times. However, more often than not, the likelihood of natural or carnal appearances leading to wrong conclusions is substantially high. It is for this reason that God told His servant Samuel:

"for the LORD seeth not as man seeth; for man looketh on the outward appearance, but the LORD looketh on the heart"
(1 Samuel 16:7).

Example Three: Many, including myself, have wrongly interpreted dreams and visions because the revelation seemed contrary to the circumstances. In my own case, I had revelations that some church workers were pretending to be part of the church but were, in fact, working against it. Some appeared outwardly to love me but in the dream, they hated me with a passion. At first, I interpreted the dream as Satan using their faces to cause strife and confusion in the church. But when the revelations continued with confirmations from other church members, I took them seriously and began to pray earnestly. Thankfully, God averted the crisis and these very people began to exit the church one after the other.

Example Four: In another instance, a young lady had a dream about a worker in my church. In the dream, the whole church was singing and dancing to God. She noticed that the worker was dressed in red and was moving around amongst the congregation. Once I got near to the worker, he began to prostrate and pretend to be "in the spirit." She noticed, however, that I completely ignored him in the dream and she said to herself "He doesn't know that pastor hates such hypocritical displays." Red in a dream can denote occultism as revealed in Revelation 6:4:

"And there went out another horse that was red: and power was given to him that sat thereon to take peace from the earth, and that they should kill one another: and there was given unto him a great sword."

This church worker had claimed to have left the occult with open denunciations but this was apparently false as he kept reading his occult books. Today, he no longer worships in the church.

A person clothed in white in a dream signifies holiness and righteousness. Ecclesiastes 9:8 reads:

"Let thy garments be always white; and let thy head lack no ointment."

The garments here are not physical; they are spiritual. The colour of the garments that you wear in a dream reveals a lot about your spiritual state. Garments of gold signify priesthood and royalty; we are rightly called "a royal priesthood" in 1 Peter 2:9. Purple denotes both royalty and authority in the spiritual realm. Be careful to take note of colours henceforth, not only of yourself but also of others. Anytime a person dreams of you, ask them what colour they saw you dressed in and the kind of garments you were wearing. Such symbols play a key role in correctly interpreting dreams and visions.

Apart from what we read in Ecclesiastes 9:8, you may be wondering how important garments are. In biblical times, which remains true today, a person's garments depict who they are — a king, slave, prostitute, or even priest. In Genesis 41:14, before Joseph was brought before Pharaoh, his prison garment was first changed. In Mark 10:46–52, blind Bartimaeus first cast aside his garment before he approached Jesus to be healed. Every blind person in that era was required to wear a type of garment that distinguished them from the lot.

"And he, casting away his garment, rose, and came to Jesus."

Your garment identifies you (Genesis 39:12, 15 & 18). Joseph was put in prison because his garment was found in the hands of Potiphar's wife. Joshua, the high priest, in Zechariah 3:1–3 was wearing filthy garments and Satan was able to resist him as a result. Wearing filthy garments denotes a life of sin and unrighteousness, while tattered garments denote poverty. Black garments in a dream denote that the person in black is being attacked by the spirit of death or that they will mourn the death of a loved one. Wearing light or medium blue in a dream usually depicts the Anointing and Fire of the Holy Spirit. Blue is the colour of the sky (1st heaven) and denotes spirituality. The Fire of God is not a yellow/orange flame but a gentle blue flame. In the natural, fire can be blue, yellow, or orange, with the blue usually gentle but hotter than the yellow/orange flames.

The timing of the manifestation of a dream or vision can also be relevant to its interpretation. The revelation could be past, present, or future, and we must be careful to discern that. In 2001, I had a dream where I saw myself raising the dead. Other people came confirming that they had similar dreams about me. Full of zeal, I went to the mortuary to comfort the family members of a dead woman who used to watch my television programme. I believed that she would be raised from the dead. After two hours of prayer, nothing happened, though her family and the mortuary attendants stood by politely, looking at me with pity as if I was a madman. Someone later discreetly whispered to me that the family was ready to go with the corpse and the mortuary attendants wanted to close. I felt really foolish and discouraged. Two years later, however, the manifestation came to pass and the first person to be raised from the dead in my ministry was a child brought to me early one morning by the parents. Clearly, in the first instance, I had gone ahead of God's timing.

Many revelations in the Bible did not manifest immediately. They were revealed but are rather manifesting in our time. We need to be careful to work within the time frame that God has given us. One of the first people to see my coming to Europe as a pastor was my mother, back in 2001. If I had left for Europe then, I would have been frustrated, discouraged, and would most likely have given up. It was not until five years after her dream that God gave me the confirmation to move.

God even determined the timing of the writing of the first edition of this book. In December 2005, God revealed to my wife that both of us would be writing books. In

January 2006, I began to write but gave up. It was about six months later that God gave us the go ahead.

When God appeared to Abraham in Genesis 15 with the promise of a child, it was not until 25 years later that the promise materialised. David was anointed king but it took about 16 years for him to ascend the throne. Joseph was 17 years when he had his dream and well over 30 years when it came to pass. We should realise that with God, one day is like a thousand years and vice versa.

> **"But, beloved, be not ignorant of this one thing, that one day is with the Lord as a thousand years, and a thousand years as one day"** (2 Peter 3:8).

God's revelations are for an appointed time and can never happen overnight, no matter how much we fast and pray for them to occur immediately. We can only pray for their manifestation but not our preferred timing. We are in the generation of the microwave, remote controlled television, and heightened technological advancements such that the patience to wait upon the Lord is sorely lacking. Habakkuk 2:3 declares:

> **"For the vision is yet for an appointed time, but at the end it shall speak, and not lie: though it tarry, wait for it; because it will surely come, it will not tarry."**

The carnal mind finds it difficult to wait for the manifestation of revelations. If you are not operating in the spirit, the time and patience needed can be extremely frustrating. You may be tempted to run ahead of God and open the door to regrettable experiences, which may even harm your relationship with God. Impatience and frustration are known to open the door to Satan, enabling him to twist the meaning of revelations and lead us into gross error.

Take the example of Abraham in Genesis 16:1–4; God promised him that a servant would not be his heir but a child from his own loins. Instead of waiting, he obliged to Sarah's suggestion of having a child with Hagar. Abraham must have reasoned that "it was from his own loins a child would come forth" (Genesis 15:4) and therefore the womb in which he planted his seed "didn't really matter." Do not attempt to help God or twist God's revelation to calm your frustrations. Today, the whole world is suffering from Abraham's mistake, which has led to the problems we have in the Middle East. We are called to wait upon the Lord to manifest His promise. Isaiah 40:31 reveals:

> **"But they that wait upon the LORD shall renew their strength; they shall mount up with wings as eagles; they shall run, and not be weary; and they shall walk, and not faint."**

We need to renew our minds also in tune with the Word of God in Romans 12:2:

"And be not conformed to this world: but be ye transformed by the renewing of your mind, that ye may prove what is that good, and acceptable, and perfect, will of God."

We should also recall past experiences where the Lord has brought other revelations to pass in our lives each time we are battling with impatience and frustration. Hebrews 10:32 and Isaiah 43:26 respectively read:

"But call to remembrance the former days, in which, after ye were illuminated, ye endured a great fight of afflictions."

"Put me in remembrance: let us plead together: declare thou, that thou mayest be justified."

Another characteristic worth noting about timing is how often certain dreams occur. Pharaoh had the same dream twice in one night, which meant that it had been established and would shortly come to pass.

"And for that the dream was doubled unto Pharaoh twice; it is because the thing is established by God, and God will shortly bring it to pass" (Genesis 41:32).

Also, the exact timing can sometimes be discerned clearly from the revelation as illustrated in Genesis 40:12–13:

"And Joseph said unto him, This is the interpretation of it: The three branches are three days: Yet within three days shall Pharaoh lift up thine head, and restore thee unto thy place: and thou shalt deliver Pharaoh's cup into his hand, after the former manner when thou wast his butler."

There is one very important thing that we must take note of with regards to interpreting dreams and visions. When God gives a revelation in the form of a puzzle, he uses men and women He wants to promote spiritually to decode it and thereby confirm their ministry. If you follow some of the examples of dreams already given in this book, you might be able to pick such instances out. For example, with Pharaoh's dream in Genesis 41, Joseph's interpretation of it was what elevated him to the position of Prime Minister in Egypt, second only to Pharaoh.

"Thou shalt be over my house, and according unto thy word shall all my people be ruled: only in the throne will I be greater than thou" (Genesis 41:40).

This was equally so in the case of Daniel's interpretation of Nebuchadnezzar's dream.

"Then the king made Daniel a great man, and gave him many great gifts, and made

him ruler over the whole province of Babylon, and chief of the governors over all the wise men of Babylon" (Daniel 2:48).

Truly, the Bible states,

"A man's gift maketh room for him, and bringeth him before great men"
(Proverbs 18:16).

Note that astrologers, mediums, occults, soothsayers, sorcerers, and diviners can never interpret a dream correctly. They can second guess but there comes a time when their deceptions are exposed. Before Nebuchadnezzar called for Daniel to interpret his dream, he first called these false evil practitioners and asked them to tell him his dream and further give its interpretation. They were, however, unable to do so. Daniel 2:8–11 gives the account:

"The king answered and said, I know of certainty that ye would gain the time, because ye see the thing is gone from me. But if ye will not make known unto me the dream, there is but one decree for you: for ye have prepared lying and corrupt words to speak before me, till the time be changed: therefore tell me the dream, and I shall know that ye can shew me the interpretation thereof. The Chaldeans answered before the

king, and said, There is not a man upon the earth that can shew the king's matter: therefore there is no king, lord, nor ruler, that asked such things at any magician, or astrologer, or Chaldean. And it is a rare thing that the king requireth, and there is none other that can shew it before the king, except the gods, whose dwelling is not with flesh."

God is the only authority on revealing deep and secret things, and they belong to Him alone. Daniel 2:22 and Deuteronomy 29:29 respectively confirm this:

"He revealeth the deep and secret things: he knoweth what is in the darkness, and the light dwelleth with him."

"The secret things belong unto the LORD our God: but those things which are revealed belong unto us and to our children for ever, that we may do all the words of this law."

Some revelations are very clear and need minimum interpretation, like the visitation Zechariah had from the angel Gabriel announcing the birth of John the Baptist (Luke 1:11–17). Others, however, seem puzzling and full of symbols requiring their interpretation by an Anointed Child of God. An example is found in Genesis 40:7–23 where we read of the dreams that Pharaoh's butler and baker had, which were interpreted by Joseph. Verses 10 and 11 read:

> **"And in the vine were three branches: and it was as though it budded, and her blossoms shot forth; and the clusters thereof brought forth ripe grapes: And Pharaoh's cup was in my hand: and I took the grapes, and pressed them into Pharaoh's cup, and I gave the cup into Pharaoh's hand."**

In verse 13, we find the interpretation, which reads:

> **"Yet within three days shall Pharaoh lift up thine head, and restore thee unto thy place: and thou shalt deliver Pharaoh's cup into his hand, after the former manner when thou wast his butler."**

The branches signified three days; the butler pressing the grapes into Pharaoh's cup indicated that he would be restored to his former position.

In the baker's dream in verses 16 and 17, there were also certain symbols revealed:

> **"I also was in my dream, and, behold, I had three white baskets on my head: And in the uppermost basket there was of all manner of bakemeats for Pharaoh; and the birds did eat them out of the basket upon my head."**

Their respective interpretations follow in verses 18 and 17 below:

> **"And Joseph answered and said, This is the interpretation thereof: The three baskets are three days: Yet within three days shall Pharaoh lift up thy head from off thee, and shall hang thee on a tree; and the birds shall eat thy flesh from off thee."**

Here again, the three baskets signified three days; the bakemeats referred to the baker and the birds eating the bakemeats indicated that he would be hanged and the birds of the air would eat his flesh. We see other examples of this in Genesis 41:15 in connection with Pharaoh's dream and in Daniel 5:5, 15–28 in connection with Belshazzar's vision.

Over the years, I have observed that there are some symbols, figures, and objects whose meanings are generally the same in most dreams and visions that they appear. Though this may be true, the interpretation of every dream and vision is influenced by the interpreter's background, culture, socialisation, and perspective, just to mention a few.

With the help and guidance of the Holy Spirit, I will proceed to give general interpretations to a comprehensive list of symbols in the latter section of this book, bearing in mind that they may have differing meanings in the spirit and physical. It is my firm belief that you will be guided by the Holy Spirit to discern the meaning behind the revelation of your dreams and visions.

Chapter 7

Breakthrough Prayers on Dreams and Visions

I cannot overemphasise the Word of God in Joel 2:28–29 and Acts 2:17–18, which I have referred to repeatedly in the preceding chapters:

> "And it shall come to pass in the last days, saith God, I will pour out of my Spirit upon all flesh: and your sons and your daughters shall prophesy, and your young men shall see visions, and your old men shall dream dreams: And on my servants and on my handmaidens I will pour out in those days of my Spirit; and they shall prophesy."

We are in the last days, and God has poured out His Spirit, witnessed in the many revivals taking place around the world. In view of this, there is an upsurge of dreams, visions, and revelations, which need to be accorded the utmost attention.

God does not want us to be ignorant of his plan for our lives and the evil devices of the enemy. As a result, we must rise up and be well versed in the things of the Spirit if we are to behold our blessings and reject the manifestation of evil orchestrations.

Having given you a firm understanding of dreams and visions, I entreat you to pray earnestly, according to the Word of God in Ephesians 1:17-18, to receive sound revelation and protection from God as you walk in His ways:

> **"That the God of our Lord Jesus Christ, the Father of glory, may give unto you the spirit of wisdom and revelation in the knowledge of him: The eyes of your understanding being enlightened; that ye may know what is the hope of his calling, and what the riches of the glory of his inheritance in the saints."**

But, besides praying for general understanding and direction from God concerning your dreams and visions, it is also important to follow up each revelation with proactive prayer. In light of this, there are accompanying prayer points for some of the most common symbols. I believe that you will find these useful as you cancel the negative revelations, which may be the plans or activities of the evil ones concerning you, or claim the positive ones, which may be the promises of God for you.

It is instructive to know that the included prayer points are not all-encompassing, but are only general and succinct guides. You, the reader, or whoever would use these prayer points, would need to expand upon them using the context of the revelations involving these symbols and by the confessions that you make as you pray.

PART II

A—Z of Dream and Vision Symbols and Their Interpretations

A

ABANDONMENT

This is a negative dream. If you dream you abandon someone, whether it be your friend or relative, you may be being warned you could lose a cherished relationship.

Likewise, if you are being abandoned by a close relative, it could mean that in your moment of need you may not find anyone to depend on.

If you find yourself in an abandoned building, it could be a warning that you may encounter unfinished projects, goals, or desires.

It could equally indicate discontinuing a scheduled event before completion, e.g. marriage, education, a business venture, etc.

ABORTION

This is obviously a negative dream.

This warns that you will deliberately terminate a blessing before it gets to its fullness. The person is being warned of a self-inflicted injury or a decision that may be destructive and abort future enlargement and growth.

ABOVE

As the Word of God says:

"God will set thee on high above all nations of the earth" (Deuteronomy 28:1–2, *KJV[1]*).

This is usually a good dream.

If you are above a mountain, property, car, etc., it could mean an unusual promotion, place of recognition, or an improvement or success in your career or endeavour.

ABROAD

This dream is a mixed bag. If you find yourself pursuing your usual business or career abroad, it could mean you will prosper in a foreign land, as in the case of Jesus:

"went there a fame abroad of him: and great multitudes came together to hear" (Luke 5:15).

---

[1] Scripture quotations from King James Version unless stated otherwise.

For example, before I travel, I see myself abroad in the country I am going to. This assures me that the trip will be successful.

On the other hand, if you dream of being idle in a different country, it could mean you are being manipulated to become unsettled in unfamiliar territory, which could lead to danger for your welfare.

Further reading: Job 15:23

ABYSS

This is a negative dream.

If you find yourself in the abyss, you are being warned about the reality and danger of hellfire so you can amend your ways.

It could also mean that you are likely to overcome obstacles and challenges before you.

If you dream you are falling into an abyss, it means you may encounter an extremely difficult situation orchestrated by forces above that needs spiritual intervention. As the Scripture says, the demons that were cast out of the man repeatedly begged Jesus not to send them to the abyss because they were aware they would suffer torment and continuous suffering (Luke 8:31).

Further reading: Revelation 11:7

ACCIDENT

From my personal experience as a counsellor, to dream of an accident is negative.

If you see yourself surviving a car accident, it could be a signal that there is impending danger concerning an upcoming trip and that a spiritual arrow is targeted against you. You need to embark on fasting and prayer before your journey.

Likewise, if you dream of an accident at home, it could mean you need to be wary of a domestic accident.

For instance, before I became born again, someone had a dream that I had an accident. I prayed and cancelled the dream. Four days later, I had an accident that almost took my life. Sister Ify (not her real name) had a dream that she died in an accident and was carried in a coffin. However, she did not pray. Six days later, on her way to Benin City, she died in an accident.

ISAIAH 54:17

Prayer Point

Pray against every projection and arrow of accident fashioned against you, and return them back to their senders, in Jesus' Name.

ACCUSATION

This is a negative dream.

Jezebel, King Ahab's wife, and other nobles conspired and accused Naboth falsely of blaspheming against God and the King. Eventually, Naboth was stoned to death (1 Kings 21:1–16).

If you dream of being accused by your superiors in your

place of work, school, or ministry, it could mean there is a conspiracy to accuse you falsely.

If your in-laws or family members accuse you falsely, it could mean they are planning to make you leave the marriage or bring disgrace to you.

On the other hand, if you are accusing your juniors falsely, it could indicate that God is revealing your heart towards them.

Prayer Point

2 KINGS 21:8–10; JOB 5:12–13

Pray against every conspiracy and false accusation of the wicked meant to bring shame, scandal, death, etc., against you, and pray that they will backfire upon those involved, in Jesus' Name.

ACORN

From my personal experience as a counsellor, this is a positive dream.

If you are planting an acorn, it could mean that whatever you are doing at the moment, despite any difficulties, will be successful and that the future of the endeavour will be an enduring success.

If you pick an acorn in your dream, it could indicate that you will come across a successful business venture.

ACQUAINTANCE

Usually, this is a negative dream.

As in the Word of God:

> **"when Job's three friends heard of all this evil that was come upon him, they came… to mourn with him and to comfort him"**
> (Job 2:11).

If you are surrounded by acquaintances in the dream, it could mean a state of sympathy over a matter that concerns you – either being bereaved or a calamity. For example, Job's friends visited him in his moment of calamity.

You need to pray against misfortune of any form.

ADDER (SNAKE)

This is a dream of deception.

If you see an adder (snake), it is a warning of a poisonous or deceptive spirit around you.

If the adder is speaking to you, it could mean you may be lured into a covenant, business deal, or endeavour that will not be beneficial to you. Such was the case of Adam and Eve in the Garden of Eden, who were lured by the serpent to eat the apple, which put them in an unfavourable position (Genesis 3:1).

If you are being bitten by an adder, it could mean that you are under attack by an enemy, or that an enemy pretending to be a close friend is on a subtle attack.

If you see an adder on your bed, it could mean that you are in a deceptive relationship.

Prayer Point

LUKE 10:19

Bind and paralyse every serpent spirit (i.e. spirit of deception) assigned against you. Also, pray against household enemies and close acquaintances that are operating with such spirits; that the Angels of God will expose and destroy them. in Jesus' Name.

ADULTERY

The Bible clearly warns that you shall not commit adultery. A dream of adultery is a caution against infidelity or immorality in one's marriage.

If you are committing adultery in the dream, it could be a warning to put your thoughts in check. For the Word of God warns:

> **"...anyone who looks at a woman lustfully has already committed adultery with her in his heart"** (Matthew 5:28, *NIV*).

Equally, it could mean that you should not confide your

hopes and fears to a new friend, as they may betray your confidence.

If your spouse commits adultery, it could mean he/she is confiding with the opposite sex.

If you have a reoccurring dream of the same person, it could mean that your relationship with them in real life has become lustful.

ADVERTISEMENT

Generally speaking, this is a positive dream. If you see yourself in an advert (billboard, poster, or television), it could mean an enhanced platform for your ideas, gifts, or products – recognition beyond your wildest imagination by strangers.

Before I became a pastor, I saw myself on a big billboard as a public speaker, advertising something on the TV. In less than three months, I began a TV ministry and became a televangelist in Nigeria. I became a household name within a very short time.

AIRCRAFT

Generally, this is a mixed bag. It relates to the greatness of your ideas, ministry, and spiritual height.

When the aircraft is taking off, it could mean that success is on the way.

On the other hand, if the aircraft is landing, it could mean that you have to be cautious of the way you are running your business or ministry.

If the aircraft is crashing and you find yourself dead, it is a warning for you to not pursue a particular business or venture blindly. You need to control your zeal or else you may meet a disastrous end.

People who have come for counselling who have seen themselves in a flying aircraft in a dream have experienced great heights in their professions.

AFRAID

This is a negative dream.

If you are always afraid or experience fearful nightmares, it is to be taken seriously. It could mean you have strange spirits around you, and if not dealt with, they may hinder the outcome of your goals, plans, business, or life's endeavour.

Consider, for example, the men sent to explore the land of Canaan (the Promised Land) who were afraid of the giants, despite God's promise to them (Numbers 13:27–33).

It could equally mean you are being warned not to allow fear frustrate or dictate your plans.

If you are up high or on a mountain and you are afraid, it could mean that you shouldn't allow your fears to destroy your big ideas and hopes. When Moses had just died, God commanded Joshua to be strong and have courage and not to be afraid for He was with him, wherever he went, while he embarked on his assignment (Joshua 1:9).

2 TIMOTHY 1:7

Bind and rebuke every spirit of fear being projected against you in order to compromise your destiny, blessings, peace, and wellbeing, in Jesus' Name.

ALARM BELL

Generally, this is a mixed bag.

If you hear an alarm bell, it could symbolise a wake-up call for you to pursue your life's endeavour, idea, or goal, which you may have been slacking on. It could also be a warning about your spiritual state.

Equally, it could mean good news, which will be heard by close acquaintances, or blessings are on the way.

ALLIGATOR

From my personal experience as a counsellor, this is a negative dream. An alligator is a reptile that has the ability to function both on land and in the water.

To see an alligator in the dream could be a warning to alert you to a decision you want to make or a project you wish to carry out.

It shows you have secret enemies, unfriendly friends, and marine associations around you.

MATTHEW 18:18

> **Bind and paralyse every marine spirit of alligator operating against you, and pray that the Angels of God will expose and destroy any secret enemy or unfriendly friend using them,** in Jesus' Name.

ALMOND

This is a positive dream. If you see an almond, it could mean your ideas will prosper and business will blossom. But then again, you have to be careful as your success may attract all sorts of people (both friends and foes) that are likely to hinder you. As the Scripture says:

> **"and the almond tree shall flourish"**
> (Ecclesiastes 12:5).

ALTAR

An altar is a place of intervention between the visible and invisible. This dream could either be positive or negative.

If you see yourself praying on an altar, it could mean you should expect the unexpected to happen in your favour.

1 THESSALONIANS 5:18

Prayer Point

Thank God for His intervention in your personal circumstances and that of your family, in Jesus' Name.

If you see other people praying naked or with ancient things before an altar, you need to pray and cancel evil decrees and curses being laid on you. As in the case of Balak and Balaam, Balaam hired Balak to curse the children of Israel (Numbers 23).

If you see yourself at your family or village altar, what is being revealed is the foundation of the problem that you need to deal with. God commanded Moses to destroy such evil altars, knowing it would hinder the Israelites if they were not destroyed (Exodus 34:13).

DEUTERONOMY 7:5

Prayer Point

Pray that every satanic, demonic, occultic, marine, or ancient altars speaking or being used against you would be consumed by the Holy Ghost Fire of God. Also, pray that the Angels of God will destroy those who erect such altars against you, in Jesus' Name.

ANT

From my own perspective, this is a negative dream.

Dreaming of ants could be a warning about your existing business or venture, meaning that you should not take for granted minor issues that may crop up, for if these are not carefully solved at an early stage, they may be difficult to tackle later.

APPLE

Generally, a dream of an apple is a mixed bag.

If you see yourself plucking apples, it could mean your future ventures will be fruitful. It could equally mean that an idea that is precious to you will blossom.

On the other hand, if you see yourself handling rotten apples, it could mean the reward of your efforts will not be worth it, as the Scripture says:

> **"the apple tree... are withered: because joy is withered away from the sons of men"**
> (Joel 1:12).

APARTMENT

This dream could either be positive or negative.

If you see yourself moving into or living in a bigger apartment than the one you are living in presently, it could mean good news.

Conversely, if you see yourself moving into or living in a smaller apartment than the one you're living in presently, it could mean the reversal of fortune.

If you see yourself in a well-furnished apartment that does not have a roof, it could mean that spiritually you are not protected.

ARM

This dream could go either way.

If an arm is holding you and you are not in pain, it could indicate strength, as in God delivering the children of Israel with His mighty arm and bringing them out of the land of Egypt (Acts 13:17).

Prayer Point

PSALM 44:3

Thank God for his salvation and deliverance upon your life and in your circumstances, in Jesus' Name.

However, if an arm is holding you and you are in pain and struggling in its grip, it could mean a strong man or woman is keeping you from realising your destiny.

You need to pray using the Word of God:

"Break thou the arm of the wicked and the evil man" (Psalm 10:15).

Further reading: Isaiah 53:1; Jeremiah 17:5

PSALM 10:15

Prayer Point

Pray that the Angels of God will break the arms of every evil strongman or strongwoman that is holding you down and hindering the manifestation of God's will and purpose for your life, in Jesus' Name.

ARREST

From my personal experience as a counsellor, this is a negative dream.

If you see yourself being arrested in the dream, it could mean you should expect a sudden problem or matter, but it will not last long.

If you see yourself being arrested and then released, it could mean you should expect sudden success after difficult moments.

ARROWS

This is usually a negative dream. If you see arrows flying or pointing towards you, it could mean wicked words and pronouncements have been released and are being projected against you, as in the Scriptures:

"bend their bows to shoot their arrows, even bitter words: That they may shoot in secret at the perfect" (Psalm 64:3–4).

You need to reverse the arrows to return them to their senders.

PSALM 64:3–4; ISAIAH 54:17

Return every arrow of accident, affliction, sickness, death, etc. that has been released against you back to their senders, in Jesus' Name.

AUTOGRAPH

Generally, this is a positive dream. If you see yourself giving an autograph, it could signify fame or recognition in your chosen endeavour.

ARGUMENT

From my personal experience as a counsellor, this is a negative dream. If you find yourself in an argument, it could mean you are agitated over a pending issue, in business or in marital affairs.

If you are settling an argument, it could mean the resolution of a dispute.

AUDIENCE

This dream is a mixed bag.

If you see yourself before an audience receiving an accolade, it could mean greatness and recognition for your efforts.

If you are in an audience, it could mean something that calls for celebration is about to come your way.

If you see yourself naked or being stripped naked in front of an audience, it could indicate public disgrace.

ASSAULT AND BATTERY

From my personal experience as a counsellor, this is a negative dream. If you are being assaulted, it could mean people are speaking ill of you. It could also mean that there are plots and plans to paint you black and hinder your progress, business, etc.

AXE

Generally, this dream could be either positive or negative.

If you are holding an axe that is clean, it could mean you are well equipped for battle, and you will be successful in whatever business venture you choose.

If the axe is unclean or muddy, it could mean you may be fighting the wrong battle, which will not yield the desired result.

If someone takes an axe from you, it could mean you are being limited in your business venture.

B

BABY

Generally, seeing a baby in the dream is a happy state.

When you see a baby, it could mean you need to focus and pay attention as you nurture your business, relationship, ideas, etc.

As an adult, if you see yourself as a baby in the dream, it could indicate an urgent need to grow spiritually as you have matured physically. As the Word of God says:

"desire the sincere milk of the word, that ye may grow" (1 Peter 2:2).

BABYSITTING

The dream foretells the possibility of a new assignment or business concern that will tie you down and demand all of your attention and focus. However, it is a project you'll have a passion for.

Pharaoh's daughter, knowing that nurturing Moses through his infancy would tie her down, hired a babysitter to shoulder the responsibility.

BAGGAGE

This is not a positive dream.

When you see yourself carrying baggage in the dream, it

could mean there are issues, challenges, and problems of life weighing you down and hindering you from moving forward in your endeavours.

BANDAGE

This is a negative dream according to the Word of God:

> **"I have broken the arm of Pharaoh king of Egypt. Look, it has not been bandaged... so that it can grow strong enough to handle a sword"** (Ezekiel 30:21, *HCSB*).

To dream of a bandage could mean you will be in a situation where you will need support or help from people you may not know.

It could equally mean that you may be in an emergency situation concerning your health and you need to pray about it.

BANQUET

This speaks of celebration and recognition of success, as in the Word of God:

> **"Queen Vashti also gave a banquet for the women in the royal palace of King Xerxes"** (Esther 1:9, *NIV*).

However, if you are at a banquet and you feel moody or detached, it could mean you have a personal regret over an issue. You are not comfortable and you cannot share your feelings with your loved ones.

BAREFOOT

As the Word of God says:

> **"naked and barefoot, even with their buttocks uncovered, to the shame of Egypt"**
> (Isaiah 20:4).

To be barefoot in a dream is not good. This could indicate that you are not adequately protected in your new assignment or job and that the business, enterprise, or ministry is vulnerable to attack.

Likewise, if you are well dressed and barefoot, it could mean that although your business plan or purpose is well intended, you may experience financial challenges that may stall you.

BARKING DOG (SEE DOG)

According to the Scriptures:

> **"Beware of dogs, beware of evil workers, beware of the concision"**
> (Philippians 3:2).

This is a negative dream.

A barking dog in the dream indicates that your adversaries and enemies are frustrated, so they are projecting fear to see if you will panic and take a wrong decision about the prevailing circumstances that you are facing.

It could also mean the enemies are reacting negatively to your success because their plans have failed.

Further reading: Revelation 22:15

BASKET

This dream could go either way.

Having a basket full of goodies in the dream could mean that you will soon have excess: your business venture will be fruitful, you will not labour in vain, and you will reap the fruits of your labour. Jesus miraculously had enough food to feed the 5,000 out of the basket (Matthew 15:37).

MATTHEW 15:37

Prayer Point

Thank God for the fruitfulness and abundance that has begun to manifest in your life, business, marriage, ministry, etc, in Jesus' Name.

On the other hand, an empty basket could mean that you may be operating under a curse or are under condemnation.

It could also mean that your business venture will never be fruitful and you will labour in vain.

If you see yourself fetching water with a basket, it could also mean your efforts will not be fruitful.

GALATIANS 3:13

Cancel and reject every curse of emptiness, unfruitfulness, or lack that is operating in your life, in Jesus' Name.

BATHING

Dreaming of bathing could mean that there is a need for cleansing and that you need to be upright in your dealings.

If you are bathing in clear, calm waters, the dream could mean prosperity and good health.

If you are bathing in a stranger's house in the dream, it speaks of contamination and pollution.

If a man or woman of God is bathing with someone who is of the opposite sex, this also speaks of contamination.

If you are bathing in a public place, this could represent exposure and shame being projected onto you.

Bathing in turbulent waters could mean a sudden calamity that may sink your business, relationships, etc.

BARE FLOOR

Generally, this is a negative dream. Eating on a bare floor represents abject poverty if care is not taken.

Prayer Point

PROVERBS 24:34; GALATIANS 3:13

Bind every spirit of poverty that is operating or being projected upon your life and return them back to their senders. Also, use the Blood of Jesus to cancel and separate yourself from every curse of poverty, in Jesus' Name.

BATTLE

This dream is a mixed bag, depending on the context and outcome. When you see yourself in battle, it is a wake-up call to put your ideas and plans into action. The need to seek the face of God before implementing decisions that may appear to be difficult or physically impossible is key, as when God spoke to Moses before a seemingly unwinnable battle against King Sihon. Only through God were the Israelites victorious (Deuteronomy 2:24).

BEAST

To see a wild beast is a negative dream. One should guard against decisions that may lead to serious setbacks or that may have significant drawbacks for your business or marriage.

Beasts could equally represent devourers after your business, blessings, and life's endeavours. As the Scripture says, wild beasts will be sent to destroy possessions and children (Leviticus 26:22).

BED

This dream could either be positive or negative.

If you are lying on a big, cosy bed, it could mean that you are at peace with the current state of your finances and relationships.

If you dream of lying on a bed, it could mean that you are laid back in regard to your ideas or projects. As long as the lame man lay on his bed, he was restricted by the forces of darkness until he was commanded by Jesus to rise up and walk (John 5:8).

It could also be that you are physically exhausted by issues that have drained you emotionally.

And if you are lying on a strange bed, it could mean that the matter is serious.

BEDROOM

This dream can swing either way.

If you see yourself in a large bedroom, this speaks of inner comfort in your decisions and security.

Likewise, when you see yourself in a smaller bedroom, it means the opposite.

If you see strangers in your bedroom, this could mean that you are vulnerable and exposed to attack, as in the Scriptures when the sons of Rimmon struck and killed Ishbosheth, son of Saul in the comfort of his bedroom (2 Samuel 4:5–7).

Further reading: Ecclesiastes 10:20

BEREAVEMENT

According to the Scriptures:

> **"Though they bring up their children, yet will I bereave them, that there shall not be a man left"** (Hosea 9:12).

To dream of being bereaved is negative. It could mean the loss of a beloved one.

It could equally imply an abrupt end of a business or relationship. The need to fast and pray is important.

HOSEA 13:14; PROVERBS 26:27

Bind and paralyse every spirit of death and mourning assigned against you or your beloved ones and return them back to their senders. Also, pray that anyone who is using coffins, pits, or graves in order to fight you or your beloved ones will enter into them on your behalves, in Jesus' Name.

BEES

This is a negative dream.

Bees in the dream talk of enemies that have conspired against your wellbeing or relationship. The enemies are working in unity to bring you down or discourage you from carrying out your wishes. The attack will come from various forms against anything that gives you joy. Only through God can you be delivered, as the psalmist said:

> "They compassed me about like bees; they are quenched as the fire of thorns: for in the name of the LORD I will destroy them" (Psalm 118:12).

PSALM 118:12; ISAIAH 8:9—10

Prayer Point

Pray against every conspiracy of the wicked ones against you; that they will be scattered and destroyed by the Angels of God, and let their evil counsel backfire by fire, in Jesus' Name.

BEGGAR

This is a contrary dream.

If you are working-class and you see yourself with beggars in the dream, it could mean that you will be in a situation or circumstances where you will need help from other people, which could come from an unexpected source.

If you are a businessman, it could mean various opportunities will open up, and you'll meet people of substance that will be of help to you.

If you see yourself as a beggar, it could mean that friends you helped in the past may betray you.

BEGGING

As the psalmist said:

"I have been young, and now am old; yet have I not seen the righteous forsaken, nor his seed begging bread" (Psalm 37:25).

Begging in the dream is negative. If you see yourself begging, it could mean a situation of hopelessness, helplessness, and barrenness. The dreamer's decision or actions may lead to a state of abject poverty, hardship, and vulnerability.

BIBLE

The Bible is the Word of God, which Christians should feed on. According to the Scriptures:

> **"Man shall not live by bread alone, but by every word that proceedeth out of the mouth of God"** (Matthew 4:4).

If you see a very big Bible and you are studying it, it is a great dream. It could mean that God will be revealing mysteries of the secret book of the Bible to you, and the Word of God will enhance your spiritual state greatly.

If your Bible is dusty in the dream, it could mean that your spiritual connection with God is becoming stale.

Further reading: Deuteronomy 8:3; Mark 12:24

EPHESIANS 1:17—18

Prayer Point

Pray that God will give you the spirit of the revelation in the knowledge of Him and His Word, and the spirits of wisdom and understanding, in Jesus' Name.

BILLS

This is a negative dream.

If you see a mountain of bills before you, it could mean that sudden help will come to you from an unexpected source.

If you are paying bills in the dream, it could mean that you should expect financial difficulties or challenges.

Prayer: See prayers on BARE FLOOR.

BIRD

The colour and type of bird define the interpretation of the dream as positive or negative.

White or colourful birds in the dream signify good outcomes of decisions and that a favourable aura is coming your way.

If you see an eagle in the dream, it signifies strength and height.

If you see a dove, it signifies anointing, as in the Word of God:

> **"And Jesus, when he was baptized, went up straightway out of the water: and, lo, the heavens were opened unto him, and he saw the Spirit of God descending like a dove, and lighting upon him"** (Matthew 3:16).

If it is a black bird or a bird of prey, it could mean moments of uncertainty and attack concerning your business, relationships, wellbeing, etc.

If you see a vulture in the dream, it signifies a bad omen.

Before I became a pastor, I dreamt that an eagle came to my right hand while a dove came to my left and anointed my head with oil. The eagle signifies that every challenge is a stepping stone to greatness, while the dove represents the presence of the Holy Spirit.

BIRD'S NEST

Generally, this is a positive dream. If you see a bird's nest with eggs inside, it could mean a fruitful business venture, as the Scripture says:

> **"And my hand hath found as a nest the riches of the people: and as one gathereth eggs that are left, have I gathered all the earth"** (Isaiah 10:14).

BIRTH (GIVING)

Generally, to dream of giving birth is good. There is a strong indication of good outcomes of business ventures. It speaks of new beginnings involving business, home, church, relationships, etc., that will bring joy to close relatives.

However, if a barren woman keeps dreaming of giving birth in the water, it could mean that she is either connected to a marine spirit or that someone with marine powers is manipulating her blessing.

BLACK

Generally, this is not a good dream. Whether it is a black car, black clothing, or anything else, this signifies darkness. It is a promoter of an evil aura.

This touches me because it concerns my late elder brother. Before I became born again, I dreamt of seeing my brother's son and I wearing black clothes and receiving my late elder brother's pension. I shared this dream with my brother and we laughed about it over a drink. Seven months later, he was diagnosed with a terminal disease that eventually took his life. If we had prayed and cancelled the dream, the death could have been averted, which is why the Bible says:

> **"My people are destroyed for lack of knowledge"** (Hosea 4:6).

Prayer: See prayers on BEREAVEMENT and DARKNESS.

BLEEDING

Bleeding could connote an affliction.

For example, if a pregnant woman dreams of bleeding, it could mean an attack on the baby in the womb or a threat against the formation or the wellbeing of an individual. You need to pray against those that want to drink your blood that

"they shall be drunken in their own blood"
(Isaiah 49:26).

It could also mean an affliction that will not easily go away unless one seeks divine intervention, like the woman who was diseased with an issue of blood for 12 years. Until she encountered Jesus, she was not cured (Matthew 9:20).

If a man is bleeding in the dream, it could mean a terminal disease is being projected against him.

If you see someone bleeding, it could mean a serious attack on their finances, business, etc.

ISAIAH 49:26

Prayer Point

Pray that anyone who wants to drink your blood or that of your beloved ones through affliction, accident, miscarriage, etc., will be drunken in their own blood, in Jesus' Name.

BLINDFOLD

According to the Scriptures:

"they had blindfolded him, they struck him on the face, and asked him, saying, Prophesy, who is it that smote thee?"
(Luke 22:64).

This dream is negative.

If you see yourself blindfolded in the dream, it could mean that your friends are taking advantage of your ignorance concerning a particular transaction or project, etc.

It could also mean that enemies have succeeded in fooling you.

Prayer Point

LUKE 22:64

Pray that every spiritual blindfold upon your eyes promoting ignorance, confusion, lack of understanding, etc., would be consumed by the Holy Ghost Fire of God, in Jesus' Name.

BLINDNESS

This is a bad dream. If you are blinded in the dream, it could mean a severe limitation and lack of understanding of life's issues concerning you.

It could equally represent your spiritual state, as in when the Apostle Paul was addressing the Ephesians about the Gentiles:

> **"Having the understanding darkened, being alienated from the life of God through the ignorance that is in them, because of the blindness of their heart"** (Ephesians 4:18).

It could also mean that in your journey through life, you will grope in the darkness.

Further reading: 2 Kings 6:18

2 CORINTHIANS 4:4; EPHESIANS 1:18

Bind every satanic or demonic power that is promoting spiritual blindness, ignorance, and confusion in your life. Also, pray that God will open the eyes of your understanding, in Jesus' Name.

BLOOD

According to the Scriptures:

> **"For the life of the flesh is in the blood: and I have given it to you upon the altar to make an atonement for your souls: for it is the blood that maketh an atonement for the soul"** (Leviticus 17:11).

Blood is the currency of the soul; a means of exchange in the realm of the spirit. The Old Testament was established by the blood of animals, while the New Testament was established by the Blood of Jesus.

Dreaming of blood could either be a positive or negative dream.

If you are taking Holy Communion in the dream, it could mean that you are entering into covenant with Jesus.

If you see blood suddenly on the highway, it could mean an accident.

If you see people drinking blood, it could mean covenant, initiation, etc. The Bible frowns upon drinking blood.

If you see people bathing in blood, it could mean evil initiation.

Further reading: Isaiah 49:26

BOAT

According to the Scriptures:

"And there went over a ferry boat to carry over the king's household, and to do what he thought good" (2 Samuel 19:18).

This dream could have multiple interpretations.

If you see a boat sailing in the water, it could signify a flourishing and prospering of your businesses and relationships, etc.

If you see a boat on a dry land, it could mean that you need to relocate your business venture.

Further reading: 2 Samuel 19:18

BODY

From my own perspective, this is a negative dream.

If you see your body exposed in the dream, it could mean that you are vulnerable and may suffer a great loss as a result of a decision you may take.

If you are looking at someone's body in the dream, it could mean that you are becoming lustful.

BOILS

This is a bad dream.

If you dream of having boils all over your body, it could mean a serious illness, affliction, attack, etc., is being projected on you from the demonic realm, like when Satan struck Job with sore boils from the sole of his foot unto his crown (Job 2:7).

However, if you are in business, it could also mean that your enterprise will suffer a serious sudden attack, although you will not be destroyed or killed by any illness or setback.

Prayer Point

JOB 2:7

Reject every projection of sudden affliction, illness, or disease fashioned against you, and let them backfire to their senders, in Jesus' Name.

BOOKS

This is usually a positive dream.

When you see yourself, other people, or your children reading books, it pertains to future happiness and prosperity and speaks of people being industrious.

If you are reading a particular book, it could mean that you are in search of wisdom, knowledge, and power, as God commanded Joshua:

> **"This book of the law shall not depart out of thy mouth; but thou shalt meditate therein day and night, that thou mayest observe to do according to all that is written therein: for then thou shalt make thy way prosperous, and then thou shalt have good success"**
> (Joshua 1:8).

BOX

Generally speaking, this could either be a positive or negative dream.

When the box is full, it could mean an unexpected windfall is coming your way.

If the box is empty, it could mean that you should be careful about any decision you are about to take, as it may be unsuccessful.

BREAD

This is a good dream. As the Word of God said:

"Give us this day our daily bread"
(Matthew 6:11).

This could represent a provision or a reward for your endeavours and the need to continue with seriousness, zeal, and attention in whatever you are doing. The need to work hard is emphasised.

It could also mean restoration, as the Scriptures refer to healing as the children's bread (Matthew 15:26–28).

BREAST

According to the Scriptures:

"Let her be as the loving hind and pleasant roe; let her breasts satisfy thee at all times; and be thou ravished always with her love. And why wilt thou, my son, be ravished with a strange woman, and embrace the bosom of a stranger?" (Proverbs 5:19–20).

This is a negative dream. If a man sees the breast of a woman who is not his wife in public, this could mean that he is being tempted and that she is attempting to seduce him – the spirit of lust is in operation. It is an exhibition of flesh.

Further reading: Song of Solomon 7:7–8

PROVERBS 5:19—20

> **Bind and paralyse every spirit of lust and seduction assigned against you,** in Jesus' Name.

BRIDE/BRIDEGROOM

According to Scripture:

> **"as a bridegroom decketh himself with ornaments, and as a bride adorneth herself with her jewels"** (Isaiah 61:10).

This dream generally speaks of marriage or relationships. The dreamer is ready and is thinking about an enduring relationship, and he or she is weighing the options and the possibilities of the relationship lasting. He or she is having second thoughts, knowing that marriage is a point of no return.

BRIDGE

Generally, this dream could go either way.

If you dream of walking over a complete bridge, it could mean that whatever your present situation, you will complete it, whether it's an assignment or journey.

On the other hand, if the bridge is broken and you cannot go further, it may mean that you will experience serious frustration and difficulty in whatever you wish to embark on. You need to pray against it.

BROOK

Generally speaking, this is not a positive dream. If you find yourself in a brook, it could mean that there will be a serious attack on your source of livelihood, and if care is not taken, it can bring dryness and frustration in your life, business, marriage, etc.

BROOM

According to the Scriptures:

> **"Either what woman having ten pieces of silver, if she lose one piece, doth not light a candle, and sweep the house, and seek diligently till she find it?"** (Luke 15:8).

Brooms connote making a place clean.

However, if you are being flogged in the dream with a broom, it could mean affliction by a household enemy.
   Further reading: Isaiah 14:23

BROTHER

This dream can be seen from two angles.

If you are happy with your brother in the dream, it could mean good understanding and appreciation of one another in whatever you are doing.

If you are quarrelling with your brother in the dream, it could mean that there is an underlying reason for your hatred that you are not aware of.

BUILDINGS

According to the Scriptures:

> **"Except the LORD build the house, they labour in vain that build it"** (Psalm 127:1).

This dream could either be positive or negative.

If you see a finished building in the dream, this is good. It could mean that you will complete any project, business, etc., that you will embark on, and there is a need to decree and declare the Word of God:

> **"And they shall build houses, and inhabit them; and they shall plant vineyards, and eat the fruit of them. They shall not build, and another inhabit; they shall not plant, and**

**another eat: for as the days of a tree are the
days of my people, and mine elect shall long
enjoy the work of their hands"**
(Isaiah 65:21–22).

On the other hand, if you see an unfinished building, it could mean that there will be difficulties that will hinder the project, business, etc., from being completed.

BURIAL

This is a straightforward dream, and there is nothing good about it.

If the burial ceremony is subdued, it is a bad dream.
    However, if people are in a joyful mood, it is the burial of a beloved one who has lived to a good old age.
    Prayer: See prayers on BEREAVEMENT.

BUS

This speaks of ministry and business.

If you are waiting for a bus in the dream, it could mean you should expect frustrations and delays in whatever you are doing.
    If you are waiting for a bus, and it is full, this could signify a missed opportunity.

BUSH

This is not a positive dream. A bush is a place of confusion, where ideas and plans are not cultivated or streamlined.

C

CABIN

When you dream you are in a cabin, this could mean that you will be in an uncomfortable situation or circumstance, which could limit either your potential or your opportunities in a current endeavour.

It could involve restriction, like in the case of Jeremiah, who was restrained in the cabin for many days (Jeremiah 37:16). It may also mean you have ongoing issues with other people and that, if you don't take care, third-party intervention may be necessary.

CAGE

From my own perspective, this could be a positive or negative dream.

If you see a cage full of birds, this speaks of opportunities and blessings that will soon manifest themselves.

If you are looking at an empty cage, it could indicate severe hindrance – your enemies or adversaries may be planning to inhibit you or your ideas, plans, or endeavours. It could also mean that challenges lie before you.

If you find yourself in a cage, it could mean that you have been bound by forces more powerful than yourself.

PSALM 107:16, 2 PETER 2:4

Pray that any cage, key, chain, or padlock of darkness that is hindering your destiny will be destroyed by the Holy Ghost Fire of God, in Jesus' Name.

CAKE

Usually, this dream could go either way.

If you dream of eating a wedding cake, it assures you of prosperous times ahead.

If you are presented with a cake by strangers, this could represent a point of contact in your life that may not be beneficial to you.

CANDLE

Generally, there are several interpretations of a candle in the dream.

According to the Scriptures:

> **"Neither do men light a candle, and put it under a bushel, but on a candlestick; and it giveth light unto all that are in the house"** (Matthew 5:15).

When you see a lit candle, it could mean that you have the ability and capacity to bring an idea or matter to fruition.

It could also mean a currently difficult situation or challenge before you will eventually turn around if you persist. For example, if you or someone close to you is sick, this shows that there is hope for revival, as the psalmist said:

"For thou wilt light my candle: the Lord my God will enlighten my darkness"
(Psalm 18:28).

If you see an unlit candle, it could mean that you are wasting opportunities before you that you could have easily grabbed or taken advantage of.

- A white candle could represent marine or water spirits.
- A red candle could represent a connection with the occult kingdom.
- A black candle could represent an instrument of death or destruction.

CANDLESTICK

Generally, this represents the altar before you, depending on the colour of the candlestick and candle in the dream, as described above.

CANE

This is an instrument of chastisement, judgment, or punishment.

If you are flogging an adult in the dream, it could mean that your prayer is working against an enemy.

On the other hand, if you are flogging your child, it calls for more discipline, seeing that the Word of God says:

> **"Withhold not correction from the child: for if thou beatest him with the rod, he shall not die"** (Proverbs 23:13)

and:

> **"He that spareth his rod hateth his son: but he that loveth him chasteneth him betimes"** (Proverbs 13:24).

If you see yourself being flogged, it could show that the enemy is fighting you and that their attack is succeeding. If serious intervention is not taken, it could lead to death. For example, Jesus was flogged by his enemies for redemptive purposes (Mark 15:19).

During counselling, a lady narrated how she was being flogged with a cane by her father in her dream. During one of our prayer sessions at church on a Friday, we decided to use a cane to prophetically flog our enemies. According to the lady, her father was rushed to hospital the following day, screaming: "Some people are flogging me!" He later died in the hospital.

It is clear that the father was using a cane as an instrument of judgment against her in the realm of the spirit. If you are being flogged in a dream, it is important to go to an anointed man of God for deliverance.

CAP (HAT)

Depending on the condition of the cap, this is usually a good dream – it speaks of coverage.

If the cap is new, it could mean that problems and challenges that you may encounter will not overcome you.

On the contrary, if the cap is torn, worn, or dirty, it could mean that temporary difficulties being experienced may cause whatever you are doing to be exposed, such as your business dealings or ministry.

CAR

In the Bible, chariots can be seen as cars. They were a means of transport for the wealthy, and all kings and those in authority rode in chariots (see Jeremiah 17:25; Exodus 14:6–7; Psalm 20:7; Deuteronomy 11:4; Genesis 41:43).

Generally speaking, this is a good dream. It could speak of your present occupation, such as your business or ministry.

If you find yourself driving a car in a new place, it could signify that you will relocate to a new environment where you will be successful.

However, if you find yourself driving a car and it gets stuck, breaks down, or is involved in an accident, it could mean that you will relocate to a new environment where you will experience challenges.

Before coming to the UK to begin my ministry, it was revealed to me by God that I was driving a car there with my family. This dream was one of the main reasons why I relocated from Nigeria to the UK in 2006.

When I came to the UK, during my forty days and forty nights of fasting and prayer, I dreamt I was driving a Land Rover towards a slope where a river lay beyond it. As I descended towards the river, I saw tire prints of other vehicles that had entered into the river. I reversed and parked my car uphill. It is a clear dream that most ministries in the UK have been hampered or consumed by the powers in the water – the strong man of the UK has to do with the water.

CASKET

See COFFIN

CASH

Generally, if you see yourself giving out cash to people, it could show that your business, which may have been struggling, will revive unexpectedly.

When you see large quantities of cash in the dream, it could represent misplaced business opportunities that could have been lucrative to you.

If you see yourself picking up cash in the form of coins, it could signify that poverty is being projected against you.

CASTLE

According to the Scriptures:

"And Jehoshaphat waxed great exceedingly; and he built in Judah castles, and cities of store" (2 Chronicles 17:12).

This is a positive dream depending on the context.

If you see a well-maintained castle in the dream, it could signify your future place of rest being assured in your current endeavour. It could also show that the success that is coming your way will endure, and your children will have an inheritance.

On the other hand, if you see an old and ruined castle, it speaks of wasted opportunities that one could regret for a long time.

Further reading: Genesis 25:16; 1 Chronicles 27:25

CAT

In most cases, this is straightforward, as a cat in a dream is a negative symbol.

If the cat is looking at you from the outside of your house, it could likely mean that you are being monitored for evil.

If the cat is in your house and you are uncomfortable with its presence, this speaks of an evil, bewitched, or dark spirit in your house.

If you are speaking to a cat in the dream, it could mean that a bewitched voice is influencing your thinking.

If a cat is aggressive towards you, it could signify that there is a household enemy who is behind your current challenges, circumstances or problems in your relationship, ministry, business, etc.

EXODUS 22:18

Prayer Point

> **Bind every spirit of witchcraft in operation against you, and pray that the judgment of God will come upon every household witch or wizard in your life,** in Jesus' Name.

CATERPILLAR

This is not a good dream.

The Bible clearly depicts caterpillars as devourers:

> **"and that which the locust hath left hath the cankerworm eaten; and that which the cankerworm hath left hath the caterpillar eaten"** (Joel 1:4).

Additionally, the psalmist says:

> **"He gave also their increase unto the caterpiller, and their labour unto the locust"**
> (Psalm 78:46).

This dream speaks of a serious attack on your finances, health, relationship, or loved ones. Caterpillars are one of the highest forms of devouring spirit.

JOEL 2:24

Bind and rebuke every spirit of caterpillar (i.e. devouring spirit) assigned against your finances, health, etc, in Jesus' Name.

CATHEDRAL

This is generally a good dream. In most cases, to see a cathedral from within symbolises great achievement before you in regard to your ambitions, desires, or business ideas. If you are focused and determined, you will achieve them.

It could also show that you will reach a peak where you will be recognised.

CATTLE

This dream could be either positive or negative.

According to the Scriptures, Abram was very rich in cattle

(Genesis 13:2). If you own cattle in the dream, it could mean that your business will expand and that you will be an effective competitor.

But if you see cattle running towards you, especially cattle that are black, they represent the wicked adversaries who want to hinder whatever you are doing. This is a dream that could be revealing confrontation in a different form.

CELESTIAL SIGNS

This could either be positive or negative depending on the context of the dream. However, dreaming of anything relating to the sky reveals your spiritual state and means you are spiritually active.

If you find yourself speaking to the heavenly bodies, it shows your level of connection with the heavenly realm, either positively or negatively, just as when Joshua was in battle with the Amorites and he commanded the sun to stand still in order to give him light to avenge his enemies (Joshua 10:12–13).

Moses and Deborah also spoke to the heavenly bodies and used them to their advantage.

PSALM 121:6

Prayer Point

Decree that the heavenly bodies will never work against you, but rather, they will ever work in your favour all the days of your life. in Jesus' Name.

CEMETERY

From my counselling experience, this is a bad dream.

If you see a cemetery in the dream, it could symbolise an imminent funeral ceremony of a beloved one, either close or distant.

In regards to your business or relationships, it could signify a forthcoming moment of sadness or misfortune.

If you see yourself placing flowers in a cemetery, it could symbolise a painful memory being activated.

Prayer: See prayers on BEREAVEMENT.

CERTIFICATE

This dream could either be positive or negative.

If you are holding a certificate in the dream, it could mean you will achieve your ambitions or goals.

If your certificate is old or obsolete, it signifies your current frustrations in carrying out your intentions.

If you are looking for your marriage certificate, it could indicate marital problems.

CHAINS

This dream could either be positive or negative.

If you are admiring chains (as in a necklace, for example) in the dream, it could mean secured business opportunities, links and connections, which guarantee expansion of your business, ministry, etc.

When you are bound in chains, it could mean your business, ministry, or relationships are under serious limitations by a powerful agent of darkness. The need for spiritual intervention is important, for the Word of God says:

> **"He brought them out of darkness, the utter darkness, and broke away their chains"** (Psalm 107:14, *NIV*)

And also:

> **"And now, behold, I loose thee this day from the chains which were upon thine hand"** (Jeremiah 40:4).

2 PETER 2:4; JEREMIAH 40:4

Prayer Point

Use the Blood of Jesus to loose yourself from every chain or rope of darkness that has been used to tie your finances, business, fruitfulness, destiny, etc., and pray that they would be destroyed by the Holy Ghost Fire of God, in Jesus' Name.

CHAIR

According to the Word of God:

"there was Eli sitting on his chair by the side of the road" (1 Samuel 4:13, *NIV*).

A chair signifies your office or position.

If you see a new chair before you in the dream, it could mean that you will be taking on new responsibilities.

If you see a bigger chair than you are used to, it speaks of a higher position.

If your chair is moved to a new location, it signifies a new place of authority.

If you are sitting on a chair comfortably, it speaks of a comfortable life awaiting you.

If you see a rocking chair, it could signify a sudden misfortune.

If you see yourself sitting on a smaller chair than usual, it speaks of demotion.

CHAMELEON

The Word of God categorised the chameleon as unclean (Leviticus 11:30–31). Therefore, this dream is negative and generally serves as a warning.

It could mean that what you are planning to execute, e.g.

a business transaction, may not be as lucrative as you think.

It could also mean that circumstances may change suddenly, and this will be detrimental to you.

However, when pointed at you, it could mean that someone is projecting misfortune.

CHASING

This dream could go either way.

If you are chasing someone in the dream, it could mean you are contending against those that want to stop God's ordination for you, as in when the children of Israel chased the Philistines and spoiled their tents (1 Samuel 17:53).

If you are being chased in the dream, it could mean that spiritually, you are weak and enemies are trying to take advantage of your weakness. You need to be more serious about prayer.

CHEATING

According to the Scriptures, God was telling Amos about the Children of Israel being deceitful by skimping on the measure, boosting the price, and cheating with dishonest scales (Amos 8:4–6). This is not a positive dream.

If you find yourself cheating without being caught, it indicates that you are taking undue advantage of a close friend or relative, and you are being warned to mend your ways or else you will be exposed sooner than you think.

If you dream that someone is cheating you, it could mean that you are becoming suspicious of that person and you are no longer comfortable with their decisions.

Further reading: Proverbs 11:1, 20:10; Leviticus 19:35–36; Deuteronomy 25:13–16

CHILDREN

This dream could be seen in one of two ways.

This speaks of an assured future, relationships, general happiness, and good disposition within your family circle, as the psalmist said:

> **"children are an heritage of the LORD: and the fruit of the womb is his reward"**
> (Psalm 127:3).

However, if a barren woman dreams of children, it could mean that her current situation is not natural because in the realm of the spirit, she is ordained to be a mother but an enemy is present. There is serious spiritual contention against her.

CHURCH

This is generally a good dream, although it depends on what is being done in the church.

If people are worshipping or doing the things of God, it

shows their state of spirituality and that they are connected to the Lord.

If you dream of excessive carnal celebrations (eating, drinking, buying and selling, etc.), it shows the church is of flesh and not spiritual at all. As Jesus said:

"My house shall be called of all nations the house of prayer? but ye have made it a den of thieves" (Mark 11:17)

Because people were buying and selling in the temple, he drove them away and overturned the tables of the money-changers and the seats of those who sold doves (Mark 11:15–17).

If you see a group of people sleeping in the church, it could mean that the elders and pastors are not serious when it comes to God.

CLIMB

If you see yourself climbing in the dream, it is all about the current and present effort you are making in relation to a particular issue, matter, challenge, or circumstance before you that you will eventually overcome, as in the case of Zacchaeus. He made efforts to climb a sycamore tree to see Jesus, despite being short in stature, and by so doing, Jesus visited him (Luke 19:3–10).

However, if you are climbing and you fall, it could mean that you will experience frustration and you may be on the verge of abandoning your ideas. It will take effort, zeal, and determination to overcome this.

Before I was admitted into university in the early 1980s, I saw myself climbing the wall of the university to join my uncle. Eventually, I was admitted into the same university that my uncle attended.

CLOCK

Sundials were used to tell the time in the Bible:

> **"And Hezekiah said unto Isaiah, What shall be the sign that the LORD will heal me, and that I shall go up into the house of the LORD the third day? And Isaiah said, This sign shalt thou have of the LORD, that the LORD will do the thing that he hath spoken: shall the shadow go forward ten degrees, or go back ten degrees?**
>
> **And Hezekiah answered, it is a light thing for the shadow to go down ten degrees: nay, but let the shadow return backward ten degrees. And Isaiah the prophet cried unto the LORD: and he brought the shadow ten degrees backward, by which it had gone down in the dial of Ahaz"**
> (2 Kings 20:8–11; Isaiah 38:8).

In general, when you see a clock in the dream, it is a reminder of an appointment. The set time concerns the manifestation of your expectations and desires.

When you are looking down at a clock or watch, it is a reminder of something you are about to miss – a promise, contract, etc.

CLOTHES

The meaning of this dream generally depends on the colour and state of the clothes.

Wearing white clothes generally speaks of a clean heart.

Bright-coloured clothes speak of favour and influence. Thus, you could be in a position of power, like in the case of Joseph who was given a coat of many colours by his father because he was more favoured than all his brothers (Genesis 37:3).

Wearing purple clothes could signify royalty, a position of rank, honour, dominion, and authority.

If someone is tugging your cloth or if your dress is being pulled, it could mean that you are being warned that a close friend is about to expose a secret of yours. It could also mean that your attitude or behaviour may expose you and leave you defenceless, as Joseph's brothers stripped him of his clothes, leaving him vulnerable (Genesis 37:23).

If the clothing is dark-coloured, it could signify burial, mourning, or an unpleasant situation.

If your cloth is cut, it could mean that there is an opening in a relationship that may expose you.

If the cloth is tattered, it could mean poverty, frustration, or affliction.

Wearing red clothes has occult connections.

CLOUDS

A dream of clouds is very illuminating.

A clear, bright sky speaks of a glorious event or future ahead of you.

A dark cloud foretells an immediate danger concerning what you are doing or about to do and has implications around your cherished or valued relationships, as the Word of God says:

"Thick clouds are a covering to him, that he seeth not" (Job 22:14).

COAST

When you are standing by the coast in a dream while formally dressed, it could mean a period of uncertainty and confusion before you.

It could also mean that you are struggling with adversaries that are stronger than you.

It could equally mean that those behind your challenges have covenants or connections with marine spirits, as the Word of God says:

"a great whirlwind shall be raised up from the coasts of the earth" (Jeremiah 25:32).

COAT (SEE CLOTHES)

This dream has mixed meanings.

If you are putting on a fitted coat in the dream, it speaks of empowerment, recognition, and success in what you are doing.

Brightly coloured coats signify favour and influence beyond your imagination. For example, Joseph was more favoured than his brothers, and as a result, he was given a coat of many colours (Genesis 37:3).

If you are putting on an old coat, it speaks of a loss of prestige or influence.

If you see a group of people putting on black coats, it symbolises those that have a pact with the devil.

If you are putting on somebody else's coat, it could mean severe limitation in the realm of the spirit. Physically, you may experience downturn in some areas of your life. According to the Scriptures, David was not convinced to put on Saul's armour, knowing it could hinder him (1 Samuel 17:38–39).

COFFIN

Usually, this is a bad dream – it represents the spirit of death.

If you see a young relative in a coffin, you need to pray against bereavement.

According to the Scriptures:

"So Joseph died, being an hundred and ten years old: and they embalmed him, and he was put in a coffin in Egypt" (Genesis 50:26).

He died at a good age. However, there is a need to pray against untimely death using:

"I shall not die, but live, and declare the works of the LORD" (Psalm 118:17).

If you see yourself in a coffin, it could mean that the enemy is using a coffin as an instrument to curse you and project death upon you.

Prayer: See prayers on BEREAVEMENT.

COINS

More often than not, this is a bad dream.

It could mean that you are being warned of impending hardship. The widow put her whole earnings of two coins into the treasury (Mark 12:42–44). Therefore, coins in the dream show an enemy wants your financial status to be reversed to penury.

If you are given coins in the dream, it could mean that poverty is being projected.

If you are picking up coins in the dream, it could mean that there will be severe difficulties in your present endeavours.

MARK 12:42; GALATIANS 3:13

Cancel and reject every curse or projection of poverty and penury that is operating over your life, in Jesus' Name.

COLLEGE

This dream is dependent on your current circumstances.

If you have passed the age of college and you see yourself there, it could mean that you are not where you are supposed to be in life. You may be yet to maximise your potential to the fullest.

If you are a young person of school age and you see yourself in the school or college you have left, it could mean that you are putting undue pressure on yourself or you have low self-esteem. You may be being warned of your critical spirit.

If you are taking exams and you have passed the age of education, it could mean that you have not dealt with certain issues in the past. You may not have addressed them spiritually, and they may be hindering you.

JEREMIAH 3:22; MATTHEW 18:18

Bind and reject every spirit of backwardness that is operating in your life, and decree that you will ever move forward concerning your destiny, in Jesus' Name.

COMBAT

This dream depends on the type of situation.

If you are always involved in combat in the dream and you do not know the others you are fighting against, it could mean that you are a hostile and aggressive person.

Likewise, it could mean that you easily pick quarrels unnecessarily and that you have a spirit of contention.

If you know those you are in a combat with, it could mean that you are too critical of people or expect too much from them.

COMPANY

This dream could go either way.

If you are in a company of people, it could mean that they are like-minded people that have the same ideas, world view, and spirituality as you. When Jesus and his disciples, in order to be separated from the multitude, went into a deserted place, still the people followed them, wanting to receive the Word of God (Luke 9:10–14).

If you are in the company of people who you do not know, you are being warned of self-centeredness and elements of pride.

CONSPIRACY

This is a negative dream. If you see people conspiring against you, it signifies secret enemies that are determined to undo you in your marriage, relationship, or ministry, as when more than 40 Jews bound themselves under an oath, intending to kill Paul in order to terminate his present endeavour – his ministry (Acts 23:12–13).

ACTS 23:12–13; ISAIAH 8:9–10

Prayer Point

Pray that the Angels of God will scatter every conspiracy and association of the wicked that is fashioned against you, in Jesus' Name.

COOKING

Generally speaking, this dream could go either way.

If you are cooking for people, it could mean that you have a generous heart and are in a position to help others in need.

If others are cooking for you, it could mean that you may need help with your ideas, business ventures, etc., from a friend or relative.

CORPSE

This is not a good dream. If you see a corpse or corpses lying in the street, it signifies a negative aura.

It could represent impending sickness and serious financial or relationship problems that pose heavy challenges.

It could also represent the death of a beloved one, as when the disciples heard of the tragic death of John the Baptist and they took his corpse and laid it on a tomb (Mark 6:29). There is a need to fast and pray saying:

> **"I shall not die, but live, and declare the works of the LORD"** (Psalm 118:17).

CRIES

This dream could go either way.

If you are crying in the dream, this could mean a good outcome, as in the Scriptures:

> **"And when the children of Israel cried unto the LORD, the LORD raised up a deliverer to the children of Israel, who delivered them, even Othniel the son of Kenaz, Caleb's younger brother"** (Judges 3:9).

On the other hand, if people are crying over you, it could

mean that they are agitated or gossiping about you.

Further reading: Psalm 34:6; Exodus 14:10–14; 1 Samuel 7:9; Judges 7:20

CROWN

This type of dream could go either way.

According to the Scriptures:

> **"Behold, I come quickly: hold that fast which thou hast, that no man take thy crown"** (Revelation 3:11).

Additionally:

> **"The blessings of thy father have prevailed above the blessings of my progenitors unto the utmost bound of the everlasting hills: they shall be on the head of Joseph, and on the crown of the head of him that was separate from his brethren"** (Genesis 49:26).

This dream speaks of recognition of your current achievements and acceptance by people that both know you and do not know you – friends and foes alike.

It could equally indicate that those that may contend with you are of different and varied backgrounds.

However, if your crown is falling off your head, it could

mean that challenges before you may completely overcome you.

Further reading: Leviticus 21:12; Esther 2:17; 2 Samuel 1:10, 12:30

D

DAGGER

This is a negative dream that carries due consequences, which in most cases signifies death. According to the Scriptures, Ehud son of Gera, made himself a dagger in order to slyly assassinate the King of Moab, Eglon, who was oppressing the Israelites (Judges 3:16, 21–22).

If you see someone carrying a dagger, it could mean you are being warned to be extremely careful.

It could also indicate your enemies are determined to destroy you through blackmail, false reports, and exposure of personal secrets.

On the other hand, if you are carrying a dagger, it could mean you are being warned that your hatred for someone close to you may lead you to take actions that will be detrimental.

JUDGES 3:16, 21–22

Prayer Point

Cancel every plot or plan of the enemy to bring about death, destruction, shame, false accusation, etc., over your life, in Jesus' Name.

DANCING

This dream could go either way.

Dancing in the dream could signify total victory over the enemies, as when the women of Israel came out of the cities dancing, singing, and rejoicing for the victory over the Philistines (1 Samuel 18:6).

If you see yourself dancing, it could mean long-awaited good news has come your way. It could equally mean the current challenges, matters, and issues giving you sleepless nights have turned in your favour.

If you see yourself dancing with a group of people, it could mean there will be a reason for a family / congregational celebration.

If people you do not know are rejoicing and dancing, it could mean your enemies have the upper hand over a current matter or situation.

DANGER

This is a negative dream.

If you sense danger in the dream, it could mean there is a need to be more careful and prudent in your actions and that projects you want to carry out must also be reassessed.

It could equally mean that an enemy is about to take advantage of your weakness in your current situation:

"our craft is in danger to be set at nought"
(Acts 19:27).

DARKNESS

This is a negative dream.

If you see yourself covered in darkness, it could mean that the spirit of death, sickness, and disease has been released against you.

JOHN 1:5

Prayer Point

> **Bind and reject every spirit of darkness, death, affliction, etc., being projected against you, and return them back to their senders,** in Jesus' Name.

Being in darkness in the dream, i.e. having no light, means you need to trust in the name of the Lord, to stay upon God because the Word of God should be a light unto your path (Psalm 119:105) in order that you may succeed in all your endeavours. You need to come to Jesus, who is the Light of the world (John 8:12). God's light expels darkness in every form of sickness, death, affliction, and sin.

ISAIAH 50:10

Prayer Point

> **Reject and separate yourself every form and association of darkness in your life, and pray that God's light of life, health, revelation, righteousness, etc., will continually dispel that darkness,** in Jesus' Name.

If you see your business premises in darkness, it could mean a state of poverty and frustration concerning your business.

If you see people holding a meeting in darkness, it could mean they are discussing and planning evil against you and your beloved ones.

Further reading: Isaiah 50:10

Prayer Point

EZEKIEL 8:12

Pray that every gathering against you in dark places by the evil ones will be scattered by the Angels of God, in Jesus' Name.

DEMON

According to the Scriptures:

> **"And the man in whom the evil spirit was leaped on them, and overcame them, and prevailed against them, so that they fled out of that house naked and wounded"**
> (Acts 19:16).

This is a negative dream. To see a demon in the dream could mean that you are under the influence of friends who do not mean well or that you have associates or friends with contrary spirits. The need for separation is important.

It could equally mean the contamination of your spirit.

Further reading: 1 Samuel 16:14–16; Luke 4:35]

MATTHEW 18:18

Bind every demonic and satanic spirit or influence in your life, and ask God to reveal and separate you from every source of those evil influences, in Jesus' Name.

DEPARTURE

According to the Scriptures:

> **"Nevertheless I tell you the truth; It is expedient for you that I go away: for if I go not away, the Comforter will not come unto you; but if I depart, I will send him unto you. And when he is come, he will reprove the world of sin, and of righteousness, and of judgment"** (John 16:7–8).

Thus, Jesus Christ's departure brought the Holy Spirit and greater blessings.

On the other hand, to be in a departure lounge in a dream and see a plane taking off without you could mean the termination of your aspirations, goals, or plans. It could equally mean that the enemy has succeeded in their evil plan.

Further reading: Luke 9:30–32; 2 Peter 1:15

DEPORTATION

Generally, this is a straightforward, negative dream. It could mean you will be relocated to a place not by choice but by circumstances or situations.

DESERT

A desert connotes dryness and unfruitfulness, so this is a negative dream. If you see yourself in a desert, it could mean that circumstances, situations, or challenges before you will require spiritual intervention. As the Scripture says:

> **"He found him in a desert land... he led him about, he instructed him, and he kept him as the apple of his eye"** (Deuteronomy 32:10).

It could also mean that help may not come from those you expect but from an unexpected source instead.

DESK (SEE TABLE)

Just like a table, this dream speaks of ability, authority, and symbolises a place of work.

If you see a big desk before you in the dream, it could mean promotion and the enlargement of your scope. It also indicates greater responsibilities and challenges in your place of work with good results.

PSALM 23:5

Thank God for your table of promotion, enlargement, blessing, etc., and claim it, in Jesus' Name.

If you see yourself under a desk, it could mean you will experience scandal or betrayal from those you are working with.

PSALM 69:22

Reject every plot and plan of the evil ones, household enemies, colleagues, etc., against you, and pray that God will reverse them upon their own heads, in Jesus' Name.

DETECTIVE (SPY)

This is a negative dream. It symbolises hidden enemies – people you associate with but who do not like you and are waiting for an opportune time to carry out evil plans they have been nursing for some time. As in Luke 20:20, the

Pharisees were Jesus's hidden enemies. They watched him and sent out spies, who pretended to be righteous so they might accuse Jesus of blasphemy and arrest him.

Prayer Point

PSALM 55:12–13

Ask God to expose and bring His judgment upon every secret enemy of your life, in Jesus' Name.

DEVIL

The Word of God warns that we should never give a place to the devil (Ephesians 4:27).

When you see the devil in the dream, it could mean you are being warned that a serious temptation will come to you. The need to be vigilant about forthcoming decisions is important because dark powers are there to hinder you. According to the Scriptures:

> **"Be sober, be vigilant; because your adversary the devil, as a roaring lion, walketh about, seeking whom he may devour"** (1 Peter 5:8).

DIGGING

Typically, this is not a positive dream.

If you see yourself digging in the dream, it could

represent current difficulties concerning your business. The implementation of your ideas may prove difficult in the short-term – you may need to work longer before you get what you want.

If you see someone digging, it could mean the enemy is working hard in order to cover, bury, or frustrate your efforts. There is need to pray using:

"Whoso diggeth a pit shall fall therein"
(Proverbs 26:27).

PROVERBS 26:27

Pray that all those digging or that have dug any pit of death, accident, sickness, frustration, shame, etc., against you will fall inside on your behalf and remain there, in Jesus' Name.

DIRECTIONS

According to the Scriptures:

"They are wandering without direction, they are shut in by the waste land"
(Exodus 14:3, *BBE*).

This is not a good dream.

If you dream of asking for directions, it could mean you are in a state of confusion or that you are procrastinating over something you should have dealt with. There is a need to ask God for guidance, for only He should direct us. As the Word of God says:

> **"I will instruct thee and teach thee in the way which thou shalt go: I will guide thee with mine eye"** (Psalm 32:8).

Further reading: Psalm 37:23

Prayer Point

PSALM 32:8

Ask God for His guidance and counsel concerning your current circumstances, in Jesus' Name.

DISABILITY

If you are able-bodied and you dream of being disabled, it is negative and could mean that you will be attacked by enemies. Your natural abilities do not show through, as when Jacob wrestled with an angel:

> **"he touched the hollow of his thigh; and the hollow of Jacob's thigh was out of joint, as he wrestled with him... And as he passed over Penuel the sun rose upon him, and he halted upon his thigh"** (Genesis 32:25, 31).

DISAGREEMENT

From my own perspective, this is a negative dream.

If you find yourself disagreeing with someone in the dream, it could represent a conflict of interests or ideas over an issue.

If you dream that you keep disagreeing with the same person, it shows an element of contrary spirits and you will never achieve any goal with that person.

In the Book of Acts 15:36–41, Paul had a great disagreement with Barnabas not to take John, also called Mark, with them on a mission. As far as there was disagreement, they could not achieve their goal, and they decided to go their separate ways. Amos 3:3 asks:

"Can two walk together, except they be agreed?"

DISAPPOINTMENT

This is not a good dream. If you dream of being disappointed over an issue or matter that you're contemplating, it could be a warning for you to weigh your options before you embark on anything. You need to seek several counsels from professional and non-professionals, for in the multitude of counsellors there is safety (Proverbs 11:14).

Further reading: Proverbs 15:22

DISASTER

This is a warning about an impending judgment based on past decisions already taken, as God speaks of about bringing disaster on people based on the previous fruits of their schemes due to their disobedience. These are the repercussions of not heeding the Word of God and His laws (Jeremiah 6:19).

DISCOURAGEMENT

This is not a positive dream.

When you are discouraged in a dream, it shows your current state of mind over a present issue or project. This means that you are focusing on the challenges instead of the eventual outcome. Like in the Scriptures:

> **"And wherefore discourage ye the heart of the children of Israel from going over into the land which the LORD hath given them?"** (Numbers 32:7).

The children of Israel were focused on their present circumstances and challenges instead of the end result. This deterred them from entering the Promised Land.
Further reading: Deuteronomy 1:21

DISGRACE

This could mean that the current state of affairs has been brought about by your actions, inactions, or failure to heed instructions. According to the Scriptures:

"Poverty and disgrace come to him who ignores instruction" (Proverbs 13:18, *ESV*).

DISEASE

This is a bad dream. You are being warned about a decision or action that may bring calamity to you and may eventually affect you physically. This can be seen when Moses told the Israelites that their failure to hearken diligently unto the voice of the Lord and his commandments meant they would be afflicted with diseases (Deuteronomy 28:1, 21–27, 35).

After Jesus healed the man at the pool of Bethesda, He said unto him:

"Behold, thou art made whole: sin no more, lest a worse thing come unto thee" (John 5:13–14).

Sin brought the disease upon him.

DIVORCE

According to the Scriptures:

"But I tell you that anyone who divorces his wife, except for sexual immorality, makes her the victim of adultery, and anyone who marries a divorced woman commits adultery" (Matthew 5:32, *NIV*).

This is a negative dream.

If you are married in real life, dreaming of divorce signifies that your domestic relationship is not stable. You must be conscious of your spouse's anxieties concerning certain domestic issues and address them immediately.

It could also mean that seeds of discord and doubt are being nurtured gradually but steadily on the home front.

Further reading: Jeremiah 3:8

MATTHEW 19:6; 2 TIMOTHY 1:7

Prayer Point

If you are married in real life, you need to pray fervently concerning your marriage. Bind and reject every force and projection of divorce, confusion, discord, and doubt that is working against your marriage. Also, ask God for peace, love, and prosperity in your marriage, and for His Holy Spirit to guide you and your spouse in all your marital affairs, in Jesus' Name.

DOCTOR

The Bible says only the sick need a doctor (Matthew 9:12). Therefore, to see a doctor in a dream has a straightforward meaning. It speaks of the state of your health and the importance of a medical check-up or assessment.

When I was still a banker, I dreamt I was undergoing a medical check-up. The dream occurred about three times. I decided to go for a comprehensive medical check-up. Surprisingly, the test revealed that I had a healing scar on one of my organs, and the doctors could not understand how that had happened without treatment or medication. God was trying to show me His miraculous healing. Strangely, it was the same condition that killed my eldest brother, which goes to show that some afflictions are projected by the wicked ones, for Satan comes to kill, steal, and destroy (John 10:10).

DOG

To dream of dogs is bad, as it symbolises the spirit of witchcraft and sorcery in operation. This has to come from household enemies that are close to you. David earnestly prayed:

"Deliver my soul from the sword; my darling from the power of the dog" (Psalm 22:20).

The need to seek spiritual help cannot be emphasised enough.

If you see a friendly, loving dog in the dream, it signifies the pretentious spirit of a close acquaintance on display.

If the dog appears fierce and aggressive and wants to bite you, it could mean that you should expect a serious attack on things concerning you.

It could also mean that household enemies hate you and that they contemplate attacking or fighting you.

If you see a barking dog that wants to bite you, it could mean that household enemies have commenced attacks against your wellbeing and the things you stand for.

Further reading: Revelation 22:15

PSALM 22:20; EXODUS 22:18

Prayer Point

Bind the spirits and powers of witchcraft and sorcery that are in operation against you, and command the Angels of God to execute judgment upon their agents, in Jesus' Name.

MATTHEW 10:36

Prayer Point

Pray against known and unknown household enemies; that their activities against you will ever fail and backfire upon them, and that the Angels of God will bring upon them the judgment of God, in Jesus' Name.

DOOR

This is a straightforward dream.

If you see an open door before you, it could mean new opportunities and help on your way, despite the fact that strong men or women have the ability to stand as a hindrance to you. For God said He has opened doors which no man will be able to shut (Revelation 3:8).

Prayer Point

REVELATION 3:8

Thank God for the doors of new opportunity, promotion, favour, etc., that He has opened for you and claim them, in Jesus' Name.

On the other hand, if you see a closed door before you, it could mean barred opportunities, businesses, etc. The adversaries at your door have shut it in order to frustrate your ambition.

If you see people at your door, it symbolises adversaries trying to hinder you from reaching your land of opportunity, as Paul lamented that a great and effectual door had opened for him, yet there were many adversaries (1 Corinthians 16:9).

In 2006 during our fasting and prayer, I saw doors open, which were favourable to the ministry. At the same time, I saw a sister leading people through another door. A week later, we noticed some members of the church were leaving.

It was the same sister, planted from another church, who was leading our members away to other churches through misinformation, until she was exposed.

1 CORINTHIANS 16:9

Pray that the Angels of God will overthrow every enemy and adversary that is out to frustrate or hinder you from fulfilling your potential and destiny, in Jesus' Name.

DOVE

This is a very good dream. It foretells the state of your spirituality and your relationship with God. A dove is the symbol of the Holy Spirit. According to the Bible:

> **"the heavens opened, and the Spirit like a dove descending upon him [Jesus]"**
> (Mark 1:10).

DOWNPOUR

This dream could go either way.

If you are in a house seeing a downpour outside, this speaks of assurance of blessings in your life's endeavours. There is a need to:

"Ask ye of the LORD rain in the time of the latter rain; so the LORD shall make bright clouds, and give them showers of rain, to every one grass in the field" (Zechariah 10:1).

However, if you are outside and you are wet as a result of the downpour, this is not a good dream. It could mean that you may experience great difficulties and regret a decision you have taken.

Further reading: Joel 2:23

DRINKING

This dream speaks of an individual's spiritual state.

If you are drinking clean water in the dream, it could mean that you are effectively assimilating the Word of God living in you. As Jesus said, whoever drinketh the water he gives will never thirst again (John 4:14). This refers to the Word of God quenching an insatiable, spiritual thirst.

However, if you are drinking bad water, it could mean that you are embracing wrong doctrines.

If you are drinking alcohol, it could mean that you are exposed to unprofitable works of darkness, such as evil books.

DRIVING

According to the Scriptures, Jehu drove when he was on a mission from God to destroy the house of Ahab, including

Jezebel (2 Kings 9:7, 20). Therefore, driving in a dream speaks of one's assignment. It can also symbolise your ideas, wisdom, and efforts towards your actions.

If you are driving a car normally in the dream, it could mean that you are in control of your affairs, such as your business, ministry, etc.

It could also mean that you will overcome challenges.

If you are driving and you get stuck, it could mean that you will experience difficulties and challenges. If someone else is driving, it could mean that you have little or no control over whatever you are doing.

DROWNING

The Bible says:

"By faith they passed through the Red sea as by dry land: which the Egyptians assaying to do were drowned" (Hebrews 11:29).

This dream is generally not positive.

If you see yourself drowning in the dream, it could mean that current difficulties, issues, or challenges that you are facing are the result of your own actions or inactions.

If someone is drowning you, it could mean that this person has a great influence over your life, making you helpless. You are not in a position to say no to their ideas. As the Scriptures say:

"But they that will be rich fall into temptation and a snare, and into many foolish and hurtful lusts, which drown men in destruction and perdition" (1 Timothy 6:9).

Further reading: Matthew 18:6

DWARF

The Scriptures categorise dwarves as unclean and not worthy of approaching the altar or to render services, such as offering bread, etc. (Leviticus 21: 17, 20–21), so this is not a good dream.

If you see a dwarf associating with you, it could mean that you have approached people who are not in a position to help you, but instead, they may make your situation worse.

E

EAGLE

According to the Word of God:

"they shall mount up with wings as eagles; they shall run, and not be weary; and they shall walk, and not faint" (Isaiah 40:31).

This is a powerful present and prophetic dream.

It speaks of strength, great heights, and the ability to overcome circumstances no matter what may come your way. Difficulties, obstructions, or circumstances will bring out the best in you.

EAR

Most people that operate in the realm of the spirit have spiritual ears. Only with these will you hear the power of God's revelations and understand what the spirit is saying to the churches (Revelation 2:7).

If your ears are vibrating, it speaks of the power of revelation. You will have the ability to hear in the realm of the spirit.

EARTH

Earth can be used as an instrument of warfare. If someone is holding the earth and looking at you in the dream, it could mean they are using it as an instrument of curse. Prophets of God like Moses (Deuteronomy 32:1), Isaiah, and Jeremiah spoke to the earth. Jeremiah used it to curse (Jeremiah 22:29–30). Jesus used soil as a means of healing. He spat on the mud and anointed a man's eyes (John 9:6).

JEREMIAH 22:29

Prayer Point

If you see someone using earth against you then you need to physically pick up earth and pray to cancel and reverse their evil projections, in Jesus' Name. **The earth is a powerful instrument of prayer warfare and blessing. I encourage you refer to my book, "Earth as a weapon of defence or warfare: How to pray using the Earth" for in-depth teachings and prayers involving the earth.**

EARTHQUAKE

Generally speaking, an earthquake in a dream is negative. It could mean unexpected or unexplainable consequences as a result of decisions you make around your relationship, future, or business.

EATING

To eat in the dream, with or without people, is not good.

Eating in a dream represents your spiritual state. It means that you are spiritually empty and you access, appreciate, or understand things of the spirit from a carnal perspective. You do not have the discernment to know what is spiritual and what is not.

But if you occasionally eat in a dream and you are a committed Christian, it could mean that there is room for contamination and your prayer life is not effective. Peter was aware he should not eat in his vision (Acts 10:14).

If someone is forcing you to eat, it shows that your adversaries are strong. The witch at Endor and Saul's servants compelled him to eat and not long after he died during war (1 Samuel 28:23, 25).

MATTHEW 4:3

Prayer Point

You should always cancel and reject every evil pollution and implantation of affliction, sickness and disease, etc, in Jesus' Name. **You should also physically take the Blood of Jesus, anointed oil, or blessed water (you can bless the water yourself using the Word of God in John 19:34) as soon as possible after this negative dream, and drink it prophetically so as to neutralise those spiritual pollutants.**

EGG

This dream could go either way.

A newly laid egg could mean your idea, project or plan has good potential and if nurtured, you will be rewarded. According to Scriptures:

> **"And my hand hath found as a nest the riches of the people: and as one gathereth eggs that are left, have I gathered all the earth"** (Isaiah 10:14).

It could also represent a seed of success being nurtured for the future.

Additionally, it could symbolise that help in cash or kind from a known source will help you fulfil your dreams.

However, a broken or cracked egg could mean a promise or idea that will not be fruitful or take off:

> **"he that eateth of their eggs dieth, and that which is crushed breaketh out into a viper"** (Isaiah 59:5).

Further reading: Luke 11:12

ELEPHANT

Generally, this dream speaks of big ideas and success.

If you are with elephants, it speaks of notable personalities in your business.

As a junior manager, I dreamt that I was on top of an elephant, which represented an unusual promotion. In real life, I was able to stop a fraud in the bank, which brought me into the limelight. I was then made a branch manager despite my low grade and young age.

ELEVATOR

This dream symbolises an unusual boost that will come your way that is not as a result of your effort. Rather, people will go out of their way to help you.

However, if you are going down in an elevator, it could mean a forthcoming attack, which will be far beyond your comprehension.

A lady had a dream that she was in an elevator when I was pressing a button on its control panel. The lady was scared, but I was calm. In real life, she wanted to stand in a political election. Although she had limited funds, I prayed for her and miraculously, she won.

EMBRACE

This dream could go either way.

When you embrace someone, it shows the depth of your relationship with them and signifies that you are being accepted despite your shortcomings. According to the Word of God:

"And Paul... and embracing him said, Trouble not yourselves; for his life is in him"
(Acts 20:10).

On the other hand, if you try to embrace someone and you are rebuffed, it clearly speaks of rejection.

Further reading: Song of Solomon 2:6

ENCHANTMENT

If you see someone enchanting your name or picture, it is a negative dream involving the spirit of witchcraft. It could mean that someone is using the power of darkness to fight your wellbeing or welfare. The need to pray using Numbers 23:23, which says: **"Surely there is no enchantment against Jacob [you],"** is important.

NUMBERS 23:23

Prayer Point

> **Pray that every evil projection and manipulation fashioned against you, through enchantment and divination, will forever backfire to their senders,** in Jesus' Name.

ENCLOSURE

This is a negative dream. It shows the degree of your spiritual enslavement. Even when you are working hard, you will incur unnecessary struggles. As the psalmist said:

"the assembly of the wicked have inclosed me" (Psalm 22:16).

Only through God's intervention can one be delivered.

ENCOURAGEMENT

According to the Word of God:

"And the people the men of Israel encouraged themselves, and set their battle again in array in the place where they put themselves in array the first day"
(Judges 20:22).

This dream is positive.

When you are being encouraged in the dream, it could mean that somebody's idea or success will motivate you to work harder.

It also speaks of healthy competition – the secret of your success will be a challenge that brings out the best in you.

Moreover, when you are encouraging others it could mean that you will be in a position to help people fulfil their goals and missions.

ENEMIES

If people declare themselves to be your enemies in a dream, it could mean that while people may not have the same mindset as you, their efforts to frustrate you will bring out the best in you.

The story of David and Saul is a good example. Saul was David's subtle enemy, yet his attempts to terminate David brought out the best in David. For example, when David was hiding in a cave while running from Saul, he wrote over 80% of the Psalms. Without Saul's declaration of hatred, David may not have brought forth certain traits and abilities.

ENTRANCE

On balance, this is a negative dream. If you see people at the entrance of your home or business, it symbolises strong men and women opposed to your ideas who want to hinder you.

For example, the house of Joseph sent spies to the city of Bethel, who asked for directions to the entrance knowing that if they got there, they would be able to strike the inhabitants of the city (Judges 1:23–25).

ERRAND

This dream could go either way.

If you are in a junior position in real life and you dream of running an errand for someone senior, it could mean that your boss has confidence in you and can trust you with responsibilities.

The prophet Elisha had confidence in one of his servants and trusted him with responsibilities by sending him on an errand to anoint Jehu as the King of Israel (2 Kings 9:4–5).

On the other hand, if you are in a senior position and you dream of running errands for your junior, it could mean that they are discreetly opposed to your vision or success. They have a hidden agenda and are not working in your interests. Furthermore, they have the spirit of manipulation.

Further reading: Proverbs 19:10, 30:22

ESTATE

According to the Scriptures:

> **"And I will multiply upon… and I will settle you after your old estates, and will do better unto you than at your beginnings"**
> (Ezekiel 36:11).

This is a positive dream.

This dream symbolises wealth in your old age and prosperity, success, and endurance in your current endeavour.

EXAMINATION

From my perspective, this dream could have various meanings.

If you are sitting in an exam hall, it could mean that current ideas, decisions, or challenges before you are being critically scrutinised.

If you dream of taking exams at a level you have passed in real life (e.g. school, college, or university), it could mean someone is relating to you based on their past impressions of you.

It could also mean that there is an ungodly foundation in your past, which you need to separate yourself from.

EXECUTION

According to the Word of God:

> **"For he is the minister of God to thee for good. But if thou do that which is evil, be afraid; for he beareth not the sword in vain: for he is the minister of God, a revenger to execute wrath upon him that doeth evil"**
> (Romans 13:4).

This is a negative dream.

If you are being executed, it shows an enemy's determination to carry out an evil plot or plan against you.

If you see people you know being executed, it could mean there will be a period of judgment for those involved. As in the Scriptures:

> **"they executed judgment against Joash"**
> (2 Chronicles 24:24).

> According to God's Word, pray that for every plot and plan of the enemy against you, those behind them will ever be a **ransom for yourself,** in Jesus' Name.

EXERCISING

Generally, if you are exercising in the dream, it could mean you need to remain focused and vigilant in whatever you are currently doing, as the Word of God says:

> **"let us lay aside every weight, and the sin which doth so easily beset us, and let us run with patience the race that is set before us"** (Hebrews 12:1).

It could also mean there is a need to keep your health in check and remain fit, for the Word of God says:

> **"But I keep under my body, and bring it into subjection"** (1 Corinthians 9:27).

F

FACES

From my perspective, this dream could be positive or negative, depending on the situation.

As the Word of God says:

> **"The LORD make his face shine upon thee, and be gracious unto thee"** (Numbers 6:25).

When you see a smiling face in the dream, it pertains to accepting who you are, what you are doing, and what people expect from you. It shows the dreamer's inner desire to show approval.

According to the Scriptures:

> **"Then my anger shall be kindled against them in that day, and I will forsake them, and I will hide my face from them, and they shall be devoured, and many evils and troubles shall befall them; so that they will say in that day, Are not these evils come upon us, because our God is not among us? And I will surely hide my face in that day for all the evils which they shall have wrought, in that they are turned unto other gods"** (Deuteronomy 31:17–18).

When you see a frowning face, it could mean that the person is not pleased with you and they are open about it.

If someone is smiling at you from a distance, but as you move towards them their smile disappears, they have a duplicitous spirit – they do not like you.

Prayer Point

EZEKIEL 10:14

At times, pray that God will expose household enemies and acquaintances who are using the faces of others, or duplicitous spirits, to fight your dreams, visions, blessings, and destiny, in Jesus' Name.

FAECES

According to the Scriptures:

> "Therefore, behold, I will bring evil upon the house of Jeroboam, and will cut off from Jeroboam him that pisseth against the wall, and him that is shut up and left in Israel, and will take away the remnant of the house of Jeroboam, as a man taketh away dung, till it be all gone" (1 Kings 14:10).

This is a negative dream. You should be aware of scandal. This dream could signify a plan or projection by close associates to bring shame to you.

Further reading: Deuteronomy 23:12–14

Prayer Point

MALACHI 2:3

Cancel and reject every plot, plan, and projection of shame and scandal against you, and return them back to their senders, in Jesus' Name.

FADING

According to the Scriptures:

"The strangers shall fade away"
(Psalm 18:45).

If you dream of someone you know fading away, this is negative and could mean that, although you think you know this person, in actual fact, you do not.

FAINTING

If you see yourself fainting in the dream, it is not positive. It could mean that you have serious doubts over an assignment you are about to carry out. The challenges have overwhelmed your thoughts and you may be about to give up. In the Scriptures, Jesus told the parable of the persistent widow. She continuously pressed a judge who did not fear

God or man to get justice for her. She did not give up, neither was she overwhelmed (Luke 18:1).

FALLING

When you are falling in the dream, it is negative. It shows that you are about to give up on something you have been working on. You want to throw in the towel and resign yourself to fate. You have effectively agreed that your efforts are worthless.

However, if you persevere, it will work out well, for the Bible says:

> **"For a righteous man falls seven times, and rises again"** (Proverbs 24:16, *NASB*).

FAME

According to the Scriptures:

> **"So the LORD was with Joshua; and his fame was noised throughout all the country"** (Joshua 6:27).

This is a good dream. If you dream of being with famous people, it could mean that you are likely to get help from a distant connection and that you will overcome the challenges before you.

FAREWELL

In my view, if you see yourself bidding people farewell, it could mean that you may be relocating to a new, secure place that will favour you. As it says in the Scriptures:

> **"And Naomi said unto her two daughters in law, Go, return each to her mother's house: the LORD deal kindly with you, as ye have dealt with the dead, and with me... And they lifted up their voice, and wept again: and Orpah kissed her mother in law; but Ruth clave unto her"** (Ruth 1:8, 14).

Eventually, Ruth was fortunate enough to marry a man of great wealth, Boaz (Ruth 4:13).
Further reading: 2 Corinthians 13:11

FARM

This dream could either be positive or negative.

Generally, it symbolises your livelihood, source of income, or workplace.

If you dream of a farm that is green and fertile, like the Garden of Eden, it is a good dream:

"And the LORD God planted a garden eastward in Eden; and there he put the man whom he had formed... And the LORD God took the man, and put him into the Garden of Eden to dress it and to keep it"
(Genesis 2:8, 15).

It shows that there is room for reward in whatever it is you are doing.

On the other hand, if you see an empty, deserted farm, it shows that you will have issues and challenges and there will be no room for reward.

Further reading: Genesis 1:29

FEEDING

This dream could go either way.

If you find yourself feeding people in the dream, it could mean that you are in a position to help those close to you but you are not currently doing so. For when you feed the hungry, give drink to the thirsty, clothe the naked, visit the prisoners, help others in need, you do these unto God (Matthew 25:35–40).

However, if you are an adult and you dream of being fed by another adult, it is a bad dream. It could mean that you will be in a position of disability and you must depend on others to survive.

FEET

From my own perspective, if you are in a ministry or a spiritual position and you dream someone of higher authority is washing your feet as Jesus washed the feet of his disciples (John 13:1–10), this speaks of empowerment for the journey ahead of you. You will have stability as you move forward and progress.

On the other hand, if a stranger is washing your feet, this is not a good dream. It could mean that you are being tied down or being seriously hindered by unknown persons.

FENCE

According to the Scriptures:

> **"And he placed forces in all the fenced cities of Judah, and set garrisons in the land of Judah, and in the cities of Ephraim, which Asa his father had taken"** (2 Chronicles 17:2).

This dream generally speaks of severe restrictions in your current endeavours. To see a fence depends on your position. If you are behind a fence and abandoned, it could mean that you may be incarcerated.

FIGHTING

This dream could go either way.

When you see yourself fighting people that you know, it could mean that personal issues and challenges you do not know how to come to terms with are making you stressed.

However, when you see others fighting, it could mean that they are contending for your attention or craving your recognition.

FINGER

As the psalmist said:

> **"Blessed be the LORD my strength, which teacheth my hands to war, and my fingers to fight"** (Psalm 144:1).

A finger in the dream could symbolise judgment, a warning, or a fight. When someone is pointing at you, it could mean that they are being judgmental and are ready to act against you.

Further reading: Daniel 5:5; John 8:6

FIRE

Generally speaking, this dream pertains to destruction and judgment, as in the Scriptures when God destroyed Sodom and Gomorrah:

> **"Then the LORD rained upon Sodom and upon Gomorrah brimstone and fire from the LORD out of heaven"** (Genesis 19:24).

If your building or property is on fire, you could be being warned of an impending calamity with a disastrous ending – the need to be careful and prayerful is important.

On a personal note, if you see yourself on fire and you are not being burnt, this could show that God has chosen you for a greater purpose or assignment. For the Word of God says:

"when thou walkest through the fire, thou shalt not be burned; neither shall the flame kindle upon thee" (Isaiah 43:2).

This is an assurance of God's protection in times of trials and tribulations, as the book of James says:

"count it all joy when you fall into various trials, knowing that the testing of your faith produces patience" (James 1:2–3, *NKJV*).

If you find yourself spitting fire in the dream, it could mean that you have a fierce spirit of anger and fury.

Further reading: Luke 3:16; Acts 2:3

FISH

Usually, this is a good dream.

Live fish signify blessings, abundance, and the fulfilment of your ambitions. This dream could also mean that a new situation will be productive. The Scripture says:

> **"take up the fish that first cometh up; and when thou hast opened his mouth, thou shalt find a piece of money"** (Matthew 17:27).

However, dead fish have the opposite meaning. As when God brought forth the first plague on the land of Egypt and all the fish in the river Nile died (Exodus 7:21–25).

If you are buying a dry fish, it could mean future savings.

Buying a smoked fish could mean you are taking a wise decision about your future.

I dreamt that I caught a big fish. Six months later, someone began to help me build my house.

FISHERMEN

Generally, this is a good dream. If you see yourself with fishermen, it could mean that you will be influential and affect the lives of many people. According to Matthew 4:18–19 and Luke 5:4–6, Simon Peter ended up being a significant member of the disciples, winning souls for Christ: **"for they were fishers. And he saith unto them, Follow me, and I will make you fishers of men."**

FLAMES

Flames generally signify the presence of God (Acts 2:3), as when the Angel of the Lord appeared to Moses within a fire

(Exodus 3:2). Also, the Word of God says in Hebrews 1:7, He will make His ministers flames of fire.

FLIES

This is a negative dream. In Matthew 12:24, Beelzebub is seen as the Lord of the flies and the Prince of Devils. A swarm of flies was among the plagues God sent unto the Egyptians, which brought about pollution, contamination, disgrace, and corrupted the land (Exodus 8:24).

This dream is a warning about forthcoming scandal, disgrace, and insults in your current endeavours.

Flies can be used to fight a successful marriage, relationship, business, etc. The enemy could be using enchantment and divination. The need to fast and pray is important.

Prayer Point

EXODUS 8:24

Pray fervently and bind every spirit of uncleanness, pollution, shame, and scandal that is being projected against you, and return them back to their senders, in Jesus' Name.

FLOOD

This is a bad dream – there is nothing good about it. It is a revelation that you will face a series of troubles. These challenges have the capacity to destroy you if not checked immediately, and it will take the intervention of God to deliver you.

As it says in Isaiah 59:19:

"When the enemy shall come in like a flood, the Spirit of the LORD shall lift up a standard against him."

Also, it was a flood God used to destroy the earth in Genesis 6:17.

When I was a bank manager, I dreamt that I was in a tall building when a flood came and filled it halfway up. However, I was on the top floor and was not affected by the flood. After I had this dream, I fasted and prayed, knowing that a flood in a dream is a bad omen. Less than six weeks later, there was a fraud that involved my branch and two other branches. All of the managers involved were sacked, but I was exonerated and retained my position.

Further reading: Psalm 32:6

ISAIAH 59:19

Prayer Point

Pray fervently against every plan of the wicked ones to overwhelm you. Also, pray that the Spirit of the Lord will lift up a standard against their wicked conspiracies, in Jesus' Name.

FLOOR

See **BARE FLOOR**

FLOWERS

From my own perspective, if somebody gives you fresh flowers in the dream, it shows the person's current state of mind towards you.

However, if they are dying flowers or are fading, it could mean that there is no freshness in that relationship.

As in Isaiah 28:4:

> **"And the glorious beauty, which is on the head of the fat valley, shall be a fading flower, and as the hasty fruit before the summer; which when he that looketh upon it seeth, while it is yet in his hand he eateth it up."**

And in 1 Peter 1:24:

> **"For all flesh is as grass, and all the glory of man as the flower of grass. The grass withereth, and the flower thereof falleth away."**

FLYING

Flying in the dream is not good. The Scriptures say:

"the fourth beast was like a flying eagle"
(Revelation 4:7).

If you fly in a dream, it is being revealed that you have active witchcraft foundations that you are not aware of – the need to separate yourself from such foundation is key.

During my counselling, many Christians and pastors have told me that they are flying in a dream, as in Isaiah 40:31. This is a misinterpretation. The Spirit can only lift you up, as Jesus ascended to Heaven; he did not fly to Heaven.

Prayer Point

PSALM 11:3

Continually pray that the Blood of Jesus Christ will separate you from witchcraft foundations in your life, in Jesus' Name.

FOOTBALL

From personal experience, this dream could mean that there is a contention concerning your destiny. If you see yourself playing football with unknown people on your team, they are angels, while those who are opposition are enemies.

I have dreamt of playing football several times with people I don't know. My team always wins, meaning that for every contention, I have come out victorious, no matter what the challenges are before me.

ISAIAH 49:25

Prayer Point

> **Concerning your current circumstances, pray that the Angels of God will contend with all those who contend with you,** in Jesus' Name.

FOREST

In the Scriptures:

> **"a lion out of the forest shall slay them"**
> (Jeremiah 5:6).

If you are in a forest, it is not a good dream – a forest is a place of danger and insecurity. You are exposed to attack by devourers, such as lions.

JEREMIAH 5:6

Prayer Point

> **Pray against every demonic attack fashioned against you: let the Angels of God scatter and overthrow them,** in Jesus' Name.

FORTRESS

This is a good dream.

If you dream of being in a fortress and you are free, this could mean that you are relatively well protected in whatever you are doing (your business, marriage, etc.), as when David proclaimed God as his fortress when He delivered him from the hand of his enemies and Saul (2 Samuel 22:2).

FOWL

See **BIRD**

FOX

This is a negative dream. As it says in the Scriptures:

"little foxes, that spoil the vines"
(Song of Solomon 2:15).

If you see a fox watching you in a dream, it could mean that the spirit of deception is waiting to strike you or take advantage of you. You have an acquaintance that your spirit is rejecting. As when Ezekiel spoke of the false prophets of Israel, saying they prophesied following their own spirit, he compared them to foxes in the desert (Ezekiel 13:4).

EZEKIEL 13:4

Pray against those around you operating with the spirit of deception; that they will never have the opportunity to strike you, in Jesus' Name.

FRIENDS

This dream is a mixed bag.

To be with friends in a happy state in a dream could mean that you will be successful in your current undertakings and endeavours and you will have cause to celebrate. As the Scripture says:

"the rich hath many friends" (Proverbs 14:20).

If you dream that your friends are far off from you, it could mean that something may make you feel disappointed in these friends. People you trust are likely to betray you. As the Scripture says:

"All my inward friends abhorred me: and they whom I loved are turned against me" (Job 19:19).

Further reading: 1 Kings 16:11

FROG

This is a negative dream. It could mean a relationship or contact will bring pollution to your state of affairs.

It could also mean the enemy is projecting the spirit of uncleanliness in order to defile your equilibrium or spiritual wellbeing. There were plagues of frogs in the land of Egypt (Exodus 8:3–7).

EXODUS 8:3–7

Bind every unclean spirit that is being projected against you, and return them back to their senders, in Jesus' Name.

FRUIT

This is usually a good dream.

If you see fresh fruit, this could mean that your desires, expectations, and efforts will be fruitful (Deuteronomy 30:9).

However, if the fruit is rotten, it could signify corrupt desires that will have negative outcomes.

FUNERAL

See **BURIAL**

G

GALLOWS

Generally, if you dream of empty gallows, it could mean that attempts to frustrate your ideas or business by those whom you have helped, or your enemies, will not succeed.

Through fasting and prayer, Esther and the Jews were able to reverse the execution by hanging on the gallows that was meant for them unto Haman and his sons (Esther 9:25).

GAMBLING

This is a negative dream.

If you are gambling in the dream and you are not a gambler in real life, you are being warned not to take undue risks over a matter you are not confident about. If you do, you may not be successful. For example, the prodigal son took his heritage and wasted it on riotous living (Luke 15:13–14).

If you are a gambler in real life and you see yourself winning in the dream, it shows you are committed to wasting your leisure time.

GARBAGE

In general, if you see a house filled with garbage in the dream, it speaks of huge opportunities you did not utilize lying before you in waste.

GANG

This is a bad dream.

If you are among gang members, it could mean that you are being warned about making a strange choice or decision over something you are unsure of.

If you see someone you know in a gang, the dream warns that a close associate or acquaintance is effectively communicating with evil associates:

> **"where a gang of scoundrels gathered around him and followed him"**
> (Judges 11:3, *NIV*).

Prayer: See prayers on CONSPIRACY and GATHERING.

GARDEN

A garden signifies your current state of affairs, life's endeavours, place of work, and present projects.

> **"And the LORD shall guide thee continually, and satisfy thy soul in drought... thou shalt be like a watered garden, and like a spring of water, whose waters fail not"**
> (Isaiah 58:11).

This dream could either be positive or negative.

If you dream you are working in a cultivated, well-managed garden, it could mean your present efforts will be bountiful; you will be satisfied with your achievements and you will eat the fruits of your labour. It shows you are in full control of your business ventures (Luke 13:19).

If the garden is unkempt or uncultivated, it shows your negligence. This may bring forth hardship and affect your standard of living.

Further reading: Isaiah 61:11

GATE

A gate is a type of altar.

If you see an open gate in the dream, it speaks of new opportunities before you (Revelation 3:8).

When you see people stand before a gate, it speaks of hindrance (Matthew 16:18).

If people are gathered at a gate, it speaks of strong men at the gate (1 Chronicles 9:23–27).

Further reading: Isaiah 45:1, 60:11

GATHERING

This is generally a bad dream. When you see a mass of people from a distance, it shows they are gathering to hinder you. God is showing you those who are opposed to you, who want to stop you from achieving your ideas, goals, or visions. For the Scripture says:

"they shall surely gather together, but not by me" (Isaiah 54:15).

Prayer Point

ISAIAH 54:15

Pray that every gathering of the wicked ones against you, whether for death, affliction, shame, etc., will be scattered by the Angels of God, in Jesus' Name.

GENITALS

This is generally a bad dream.

When you see the genitals of someone you do not know in the dream, it is the spirit of lust. The enemy is projecting this immorality to defile you. As the Scripture says:

"There she lusted after her lovers, whose genitals..." (Ezekiel 23:20, *NIV*).

If you see the genitals of someone you know, and the dream has occurred more than once, it could mean that you are being lustful towards that person.

Bind every spirit of lust, nakedness, and uncleanness that is being projected against you, in Jesus' Name.

GHOST

This is generally a bad dream.

If you dream of a ghost, it could mean that you are being warned to be cautious of fear and that your imagination concerning a disturbing present matter or issue is unfounded. Consider the disciples in Matthew 14:26, *NIV*:

> **"When the disciples saw him walking on the lake, they were terrified. 'It's a ghost,' they said, and cried out in fear."**

GIANT

This dream is a mixed bag.

If giants in a dream surround you and you are not afraid, it speaks of guardian angels.

It equally could mean that you will take giant strides in your endeavours and be successful.

If you see a giant in the dream and you are scared or running away, it could mean that you doubt your ability to undertake a giant stride necessary for your success, goal, or achievement.

As when spies were sent to the promised land of Canaan their report was:

> **"And there we saw the giants, the sons of Anak, which come of the giants: and we were in our own sight as grasshoppers"** (Numbers 13:33).

They doubted God's ability and theirs and refused to enter the Promised Land.

If a giant is pursuing you or one confronts you, it could mean that those who are stronger than you want to frustrate your efforts.

Further reading: 1 Samuel 17:1–58

MATTHEW 12:29

Prayer Point

Bind every spiritual giant, strongman, or strongwoman that is assigned against you, and command the Angels of God to overthrow them, in Jesus' Name.

GIFTS

This is generally a good dream.

If you are giving someone a gift in the dream, it could mean that you are going to receive unusual favour from people both far and near. Your gifts will bring you before great men:

> **"A man's gift maketh room for him, and bringeth him before great men"**
> (Proverbs 18:16).

However, if you are receiving a gift, it could mean that someone has remembered your past good deed to them.

If you do not appreciate the gift, it could mean that somebody will show you ingratitude for good you have done.

GOLD

This is generally a good dream. If you are handling gold or have anything to do with it, it could mean that your present challenges will be successful, in spite of what may come your way to derail your plans.

> **"That the trial of your faith, being much more precious than of gold"** (1 Peter 1:7).

It could equally represent possessions that are durable. Abraham was very rich in gold, silver, and cattle (Genesis 13:2).

GOSSIP

Generally, this is not a good dream. If the gossip is about you, it pertains to positivity – where the enemy thought you would fail, you succeeded.

However, if you are among those gossiping, you are being warned to bridle your tongue.

> **"And the tongue is a fire, a world of iniquity: so is the tongue among our members, that it defileth the whole body, and setteth on fire the course of nature; and it is set on fire of hell"** (James 3:6).

GRADUATION

Generally, this dream indicates a successful outcome in whatever you are about to do. Others will acclaim your efforts.

GRAPES

This speaks of a restoration of fellowship. As the Scripture says:

"Behold, the days come, saith the LORD, that the plowman shall overtake the reaper, and the treader of grapes him that soweth seed" (Amos 9:13).

Further reading: Genesis 40:9–11

GRASS

This is generally a good dream.

Grass speaks of minor issues or challenges that you will eventually overcome if you give them attention spiritually or otherwise.

If you dream of seeing grass in a compound being cut by someone other than you, it could mean that what you desire will come but not by your efforts.

Further reading: Deuteronomy 11:15, 32:2; Job 5:2

GRASSHOPPER

This is not a good dream. To dream of grasshoppers symbolises devourers in your field and warns of a serious attack in areas of your finances and business.

Prayer Point

MALACHI 3:11

Bind and rebuke every spirit of grasshopper and locust (devouring spirits) assigned against your finances, health, blessing, destiny, etc, in Jesus' Name.

GRAVE

To dream of a grave is a negative dream that has to do with the death of an acquaintance.

If the grave is freshly dug, it could mean that enemies have embarked on satanic or evil acts (Hosea 13:14).

If it is an old grave, it could mean that the enemy has not relented in their evil plot against you or your beloved ones.

If you see the grave of a dead relative in the dream, it could mean the invocation of their spirit by those who hate you in order to fight you.

In 2003, after answering the Call of God upon my life, I dreamt of several graves, so I began to pray and cancel the spirit of death in my immediate family. Two months later, I came home for Christmas. I hosted a buffet at my family's house for some guests who came from abroad. Because I had just finished fasting and prayer for the New Year, I did not have the appetite to eat – everybody ate except for me. They ate from every dish, except a certain pot of stew with assorted meats. I decided to take it to my home in the town, but my wife also desired to take the stew and sent a driver to pick it up. I refused and said that I would bring it myself the next day to ensure that I would have a large enough portion of it after arriving. The day after, the stew was found to be dissolved into powder. Apparently, this dish was poisoned, by whom we cannot tell.

Further reading: Job 24:19; Psalm 31:17

HOSEA 13:14

Bind and paralyse every spirit of death and mourning assigned against you or your beloved ones, and return them back to their senders, in Jesus' Name.

PROVERBS 26:27

Decree that anyone who is using coffins, pits, or graves in order to fight you or your beloved ones will enter into them on your behalves, in Jesus' Name.

H

HAIR

According to the Scriptures, hair signifies glory (1 Corinthians 11:15). However, a dream concerning hair connotes different meanings.

If your hair is long, thick, and healthy in the dream, it speaks of self-actualisation, contentment, and an increase in self-worth.

If your hair was shaven and it begins to grow, it could mean that you will recover from difficulties in a successful and rewarding way, as in the case of Samson, whose hair was the source of his strength. When it was shaven, he lost his capabilities, rendering him powerless. Eventually, his hair grew, enabling him to take revenge on the Philistines (Judges 16:19–22).

If your hair is being shaved in the dream, it could mean that you are under serious spiritual attack and the enemy wants to render you powerless.

If your hair is falling out, you could be being warned of a sudden sickness that may come through spiritual attack. The need to pray is important.

Prayer Point

1 SAMUEL 14:45

Pray fervently against all those who want to destroy your health, glory, destiny, spiritual cover, etc.; let the Angels of God overthrow them, in Jesus' Name.

Prayer Point

MATTHEW 10:30

Pray that whoever has taken your hair for evil, to fight your glory, to exchange your destiny, etc., will never live to execute their wicked plans; let the Angels of God execute judgment upon them, in Jesus' Name.

HAIRDRESSER

This is usually not a good dream. When someone is braiding your hair without your consent, it could mean a trusted friend has revealed something personal about you and is gossiping.

Like in the case of Samson and his wife Delilah:

"and she caused him to shave off the seven locks of his head; and she began to afflict him, and his strength went from him"
(Judges 16:19).

HALL

A hall is a place of judgment. As in the case of Jesus and Paul, both were accused and judged in a hall (Mark 15:16; Acts 23:35).

When you see yourself summoned to an empty hall, it is an indication that you may face some doubts and problems concerning current endeavours.

MARK 15:16; ACTS 23:35

Prayer Point

Generally, you should pray against those invoking your spirit into those halls for evil and cancel and reverse any evil judgment (death, sickness, affliction, etc.) that has been made against you, in Jesus' Name.

HAND

This dream could either be positive or negative.

If you dream that a hand is holding you firmly and you are calm and not agitated, it shows that the hand of God is upon you. As Jesus said in the book of John, no man is able to pluck us out of God's hands. God's hand here speaks of protection (John 10:28–29).

JOHN 10:28–29

Prayer Point

> Thank God that, because you are in the hollow of His hand through our Lord Jesus Christ, none shall ever be able to pluck out **your life or destiny,** in Jesus' Name.

If you see an aggressive hand stretched towards you and you are afraid, it is an evil hand. You are being warned that the enemy wants to strike your business venture, health, beloved ones, etc. God stretched his hand against the Egyptians, striking them with ten plagues (Exodus 3:20).

1 KINGS 13:4

Prayer Point

> Pray that any wicked hand that is stretched out against your health, business, beloved ones, etc., or holding your destiny, will **wither and dry,** in Jesus' Name.

HANDBAG

Generally, if you are looking for your handbag in the dream, it could mean someone close to you might take undue advantage of you to steal what is dear to you.

HANDCUFF

This is a negative dream. From my own understanding, this could mean being demobilised by a strong man or woman.
Further reading: Psalm 107:16; Isaiah 45:2

Prayer Point

JEREMIAH 40:4; MATTHEW 18:18

You need to loose yourself from every spiritual bondage, and pray that any handcuff, chain, rope, or padlock tying your hands spiritually, financially, etc., would be destroyed by the Holy Ghost Fire of God, in Jesus' Name.

HANDSHAKE

From my own perspective, shaking someone's hand warmly in a dream could mean acceptance.

HANDWRITING

"Then... this writing was written... MENE; God hath numbered thy kingdom, and finished it" (Daniel 5:24–26).

If you see illegible handwriting in a dream, it could mean that someone has employed the services of others to undermine your current success. It is important to pray using Colossians 2:14: **"Blotting out the handwriting of ordinances that was against us."**

COLOSSIANS 2:14; ISAIAH 10:1

Use the Blood of Jesus Christ to cancel and reverse every evil decree, petition, and handwriting of ordinances fashioned against you, in Jesus' Name.

HARVEST

Harvest is a time when what you have sown comes to fruition – a time of manifestation (2 Corinthians 9:10).

To dream of a harvest could show the need for you to work harder, as attempts are being made by enemies to frustrate whatever you are doing. As the Scripture says:

> **"Pray ye therefore the Lord of the harvest, that he will send forth labourers into his harvest"** (Matthew 9:38).

Further reading: Exodus 34:21; John 4:35–36

> Thank God because the time of the manifestation of your blessings and expectations has come to fruition. Therefore, use the Name and the Blood of Jesus to command the Angels of God to help you possess your harvest, and to also contend with all those who will ever attempt to hinder it, in Jesus' Name.

HAT

See **CAP**

HEAVEN

"And they heard a great voice from heaven saying unto them, Come up hither. And they ascended up to heaven in a cloud; and their enemies beheld them" (Revelation 11:12).

This is generally a good dream. It shows your current spiritual state and your heart's desire in the realm of the spirit.

Before I became a pastor, I dreamt I was climbing up the back of the world, and many people were following me. However, I could not turn back due to the steepness of the climb. I got to the peak of the world and discovered a window, and I was cautious not to fall. I was contemplating whether to jump in or to put one leg in first to ensure that I would not slip or fall off.

A second dream about Heaven was revealed to my wife. In this dream, I was telling her of another dream that I had where I went to see God, and He said that He was impressed with me and that I would be surprised with what He had in store for me. However, He did say that I had a fault, and I replied to God that He did the same thing in the Bible. From the way I responded, my wife felt agitated, so she asked me how God responded to my answer, and I replied that God began to laugh.

A third dream was revealed to the women's leader in our church in London, where she was told I was among those with the highest record in Heaven.

HELL

This is generally not a good dream. It is a warning to mend your ways and seek the face of the Lord. Your actions or inactions may lead you to an early death.

> **"But the fearful, and unbelieving, and the abominable, and murderers, and whoremongers, and sorcerers, and idolaters, and all liars, shall have their part in the lake which burneth with fire and brimstone: which is the second death"** (Revelation 21:8).

Before I became born again, I dreamt I was falling, stage by stage, into what I now know as the bottomless pit. I woke up sweating, and a voice told me, "That is how people die and go to Hell, thinking that they are still asleep."

Further reading: Matthew 10:28

HIGHWAY

A highway in the dream has strong spiritual meaning.

If the highway is lonely and you are wearing white clothing and/or walking with a Bible, it could show that you are walking on the path of righteousness, which is paved by God – this leads to Heaven. The Bible says:

> **"And an highway shall be there, and a way, and it shall be called The way of holiness"** (Isaiah 35:8).

If the highway is busy with people and cars, it could show that you are on the highway of man, which is paved by man – this leads to Hell. Like the Scripture says:

> **"There is a way which seemeth right unto a man, but the end thereof are the ways of death"** (Proverbs 14:12).

There is need to be careful.

Further reading: Isaiah 40:3; Judges 20:32, 45

HILL

The interpretation of this dream depends on where you are on the hill are and what you are doing on it.

If you are climbing a hill, this could mean that despite challenges, you are very determined to overcome issues and challenges before you.

If you are standing on top of a hill, this tells of assured victory despite what will be thrown at you.

"Ye are the light of the world. A city that is set on an hill cannot be hid" (Matthew 5:14).

If you are standing before a hill in the dream, you may be contemplating and focusing on difficulties and issues before you.

Further reading: Psalm 121:1, 24:3

HISSING

Generally, hissing in the dream is not very positive.

If you find yourself hissing in the dream, it could mean that you have given up on the issues and challenges facing you.

When someone hisses at you, it could mean that they are jealous or envious of your achievements.

Further reading: 1 Kings 9:8; Jeremiah 19:8; Lamentations 2:16

HOLE

Holes in a dream are negative.

They could represent a trap. It is likely that the enemy wants to set a trap, and this dream is warning you of your enemy's plots and plans. As the Word of God says:

> **"But this is a people robbed and spoiled; they are all of them snared in holes"**
> (Isaiah 42:22).

If you find yourself in a hole, it shows that the enemy has succeeded in frustrating you.
   Prayer: See prayers on DIGGING.

HOLIDAY

This is a straightforward dream. When you are on holiday in a dream, it shows that there is a need for you to give yourself rest, just as the Jews rested from their enemies in Esther 9:22.

HOME

This is a pleasant dream. It shows that whatever you are doing or planning will be a blessing not only to you but also to others.

HONEY

This could mean that the stress and difficulty you are going through will have a happy ending. If you don't give up, all will be well. The children of Israel went through difficulties in the wilderness, and eventually, they got to the land flowing with milk and honey, which God had promised them (Exodus 13:5).

It could also indicate healing. According to 1 Samuel 14:25, 27, *NASB*:

> **"there was honey upon the ground... and dipped it in the honeycomb, and put his hand to his mouth, and his eyes brightened."**

Further Reading: 2 Samuel 17:29

HORSE

> **"Hast thou given the horse strength?"**
> (Job 39:19).

This speaks of might. If you are riding a horse in the dream, this could mean that God is helping you through your journey of life.

Further reading: Proverbs 21:31; 1 Kings 4:26–27

HOSPITAL

Generally, when you find yourself in hospital in a dream, the enemy is trying to attack your wellbeing. You must watch the state of your health.

DEUTERONOMY 7:15

Reject every evil projection and manipulation against your health (sickness, affliction, terminal diseases) and command them back to their senders, in Jesus' Name.

HOTEL (INN)

This is typically a positive dream. When you see yourself in a hotel, this symbolises the assurance of comfort and wellbeing.

Further reading: Luke 2:7, 10:34–35; Genesis 42:27

HOUSE

Generally speaking, when you find yourself in a completed house in a dream, it means that any project you embark on and follow through with prayer will be successful.

Further Reading: Psalm 127:1; Proverbs 14:1; Proverbs 24:3

HUGGING (SEE EMBRACE)

From my perspective, this represents a happy ending of a matter that has been stressful to you.

HUNTER

This is a negative dream, warning you that a skilful and sophisticated enemy is after your life and wellbeing. They are biding their time to strike. For the Word of God says in Proverbs 6:5: **"Deliver thyself as a roe from the hand of the hunter."**

PSALM 140:4

Prayer Point

> **Pray that the Angels of God will pursue and overthrow every violent person after your wellbeing and destiny,** in Jesus' Name.

HURRICANE (SEE STORM)

From my counselling experience, this dream warns of a sudden and unexpected calamity that will be devastating to your personal business. The need to be vigilant is vital.

Further reading: Job 27:21; Isaiah 25:4, 28:2

ISAIAH 25:4

Prayer Point

> **Cancel and reject every calamity being projected against your personal endeavours and wellbeing,** in Jesus' Name.

HUSBAND

From my own perspective, if an unmarried woman dreams of a husband, this symbolises a spirit husband – one needs to separate from him through prayer.

Equally, this could mean that the dreamer had been dedicated to a family idol in the past and needs to deal with this issue.

But if a married woman dreams of living as a single woman with no husband, this is a bad dream. She should pray against being separated. Like the Scripture says in John 4:18:

> "For thou hast had five husbands; and he whom thou now hast is not thy husband: in that saidst thou truly."

2 CORINTHIANS 6:14–17

Prayer Point

Bind every spirit husband operating in your life. Also, use the Blood of Jesus Christ to sever every foundational link and soul tie with spirit husbands in your life, and separate yourself from them, in Jesus' Name.

I

IDOL

This is a negative dream.

To dream of idols symbolises demons or demonic forces.

When the idol is speaking to you in the dream, it has to do with your foundational issues.

When you are before an idol and you feel strange, it could mean that enemies have used your name or picture for invocation.

King Asa of Judah was loyal to God and destroyed the idols that his grandmother made. In order to go far in life, one has to destroy every family idol.

"Asa destroyed her idol, and burnt it"
(1 Kings 15:13).

DEUTERONOMY 7:5

Prayer Point

Pray that the Holy Ghost Fire of God will consume every idol on assignment against you, or that is operating in your foundation, in Jesus' Name.

ILLNESS (SICKNESS, INFIRMITY)

This dream is negative.

To be ill in a dream could mean that the enemy is planning to attack your health and wellbeing. The need to fast and pray is important, for God sustains us on our sick bed and restores us from the bed of illness (Psalm 41:3).

It could equally mean you are burdened with an issue or tired of a reoccurring circumstance that is affecting your wellbeing.

Further reading: Isaiah 53:5; Matthew 4:23; Mark 5:26

Prayer Point

1 PETER 2:24

Reject every projection of sickness and disease using the Word of God in 1 Peter 2:24, in Jesus' Name.

INCENSE

This is a clear case of a demonic atmosphere. If you see people around an altar of incense, it signifies wicked ones practising incantation and divination against you. Like the Scripture says, the women burned incense to the Queen of Heaven (Jeremiah 44:19).

> **Use the Blood of Jesus to cancel every evil incense that has been released against you, and command the East wind to return the projections back to their senders,** in Jesus' Name.

INFANT

See **CHILDREN**

INFIRMARY

See **HOSPITAL**

INITIATION

From a general perspective, this is a negative dream.

If you are the one being initiated by people you do not know, it could mean that you may not actually know close friends as well as you think you do.

If you see someone else you know being initiated it could mean they are into certain things. You do not have a true picture of who they are.

ISAIAH 28:18

Prayer Point

> **Cancel and reject every satanic, demonic, occultic, or marine initiation that has been made over your life, knowingly or unknowingly,** in Jesus' Name.

INJECTION

Generally, to be injected in the dream is not good. It could signal the beginning of an affliction or sickness through a spiritual attack. It will take an intervention to be delivered from such affliction.

Two years into my ministry, I dreamt that a member's husband, who was a doctor, was trying to inject me. I was refusing and struggling. As I was saying no, I woke up, and prayed against the enemy. Shortly after, his wife's attendance at my church became an issue at home and she could not attend as frequently as before. After a while, she stopped coming altogether. The ministration I received was that the man was trying to afflict me and he failed.

The wife of a distant friend revealed to me, upon his death, that he had a reoccurring dream of being injected. These dreams were neither taken seriously nor addressed through effective fasting and prayers. In the end, he died of heart attack.

There seems to be a correlation between people seeing themselves being injected in a dream and physical manifestations of severe afflictions.

1 PETER 2:24; MATTHEW 15:13

Prayer Point

Pray seriously against every evil implantation of sickness and disease using the Word of God in 1 Peter 2:24, and command them to be uprooted and to be sent back to their senders, in Jesus' Name.

INJURY

This is generally a bad dream. To sustain an injury in a dream is a serious matter and could mean that an enemy has succeeded in their plot against you.

The need to seek God's restorative power is important, for He restored Israel from captivity and injury (Jeremiah 30:12–13).

It could equally mean that you may do yourself harm by making a hasty decision.

JEREMIAH 30:12–13, 16

Cancel and reject every plot of the wicked ones against your wellbeing and destiny. Also, pray that God will heal your circumstances and reverse all the evil that they have done, in Jesus' Name.

INSECT

The Bible clearly refers to insects as an abomination. According to Leviticus 11:23:

"But all other flying creeping things, which have four feet, shall be an abomination unto you."

This dream has mixed meanings.

If you see a dead insect in the dream, it could mean the attempts of an enemy to hinder you failed.

If you have insects all over your house, it could mean you are under demonic attack and an enemy wants to afflict your household.

If the insects are in your work premises, it could mean that your business may suffer severe downturn or loss of earnings.

Further reading: Exodus 8:24; Deuteronomy 14:19; Psalm 78:45

EXODUS 8:24

Prayer Point

Bind and rebuke every demonic force assigned against your dwelling, work, business place, etc, in Jesus' Name.

INTERCOURSE

See **SEX**

INTERVIEW

This is generally a good dream.

If you have a job in real life and you dream of being interviewed, you may be on track for promotion. It could also mean that challenges you are facing may be rewarding in the end.

On the other hand, if you do not have a job and you are being interviewed, it may take some time to gain employment.

INVITATION

Usually, this is a positive dream.

If you receive an invitation from people you do not know, there may be a sudden positive change and new levels of connections in your current dealings.

If you receive an invitation from people you do know, it could mean there is a need to tread softly on a forthcoming matter concerning your friends or relatives. Like Haman and Esther in Esther 5:12:

> **"Haman said moreover, Yea, Esther the queen did let no man come in with the king unto the banquet that she had prepared but myself; and to morrow am I invited unto her also with the king."**

J

JACKPOT

Generally, this dream could go either way. To dream of winning a jackpot could mean you are putting your trust into something you have little or no control over.

It could also be a warning that you are daydreaming. The need to be realistic over financial or social matters cannot be overemphasised.

Equally, it could mean that a windfall is within reach.

JACUZZI

From my own perspective, this is a positive dream. It speaks of comfort and luxury.

JAIL (PRISON)

To be in jail in the dream is not good. It could mean you are being warned to watch your actions that may bring untold hardship to you and your beloved ones. For although the apostles were doing the work of God, they were arrested and put in jail (Acts 5:18).

Further reading: Acts 12:5; Isaiah 61:1

JAVELIN

A javelin in a dream symbolises assassination.

To see a javelin being thrown at you could mean that an enemy is determined to destroy your good name and business through character assassination. Consider Saul who saw David as a rival of his son. Saul threw a javelin at David because he thought that if he was alive, his son Jonathan would never be king (1 Samuel 20:33).

It could also mean that subtle devices are being employed to destroy you.

JOB 5:12

Prayer Point

Pray that God will overturn every secret plot of the enemy to assassinate your good name and endeavours, or to destroy you, in Jesus' Name.

JEALOUSY

Generally speaking, if you dream of being jealous of an associate or friend, it could mean that you are determined to work hard and excel in your current endeavour.

Further reading: Deuteronomy 29:20; 1 Kings 14:22

JESUS

This is a great dream.

If you are not born again and see Jesus in a dream, it could mean that you are being beckoned unto salvation. The need to mend your ways is important. You need to take charge of your current spiritual state.

However, if you are born again and Jesus appears in your dream, it could mean that your current spiritual state with God is secured.

JEWELS

This is a positive dream.

If you dream of receiving jewels, it could mean that you may receive a gift from a distant connection – someone who is not close to you. Like the Egyptians and the children of Israel:

> **"And the children of Israel did according to the word of Moses; and they borrowed of the Egyptians jewels of silver, and jewels of gold, and raiment"** (Exodus 12:35).

If you are putting on jewels, you could be being assured that your hard work and labour will yield much fruit. Like Ezekiel 16:11–13 says:

> **"I decked thee also with ornaments, and I put bracelets upon thy hands, and a chain on thy neck... and thou wast exceeding beautiful, and thou didst prosper into a kingdom."**

JOURNEY

From my own perspective, if you see yourself embarking on a journey in the dream, it could mean that you are about to take decisions, or act on matters, that you are not very familiar with.

It could also mean that you are about to enter into unfamiliar territory in your business or another situation, as in the case of the prodigal son who embarked on a journey to an unfamiliar domain, thereby squandering all his inheritance (Luke 15:13).

Further reading: Numbers 10:29

JUDGE

Generally speaking, if you see a judge in a dream, it is a revelation that there is a spiritual giant, or a strong man or woman, behind your issues.

However, if you are arguing with a judge, it could mean that your enemy is getting desperate and frustrated.

K

KEY

This dream has mixed meanings.

To dream about keys is both physical and spiritual because keys symbolise openings and closings in the future.

If you are given a key in the dream, it speaks of a higher assignment, more responsibility, or improved influence. As the Word of God says in Isaiah 22:22:

> **"And the key of the house of David will I lay upon his shoulder; so he shall open, and none shall shut; and he shall shut, and none shall open."**

If you are giving keys to others, it shows recognition and acceptance of the recipient.

If keys are taken away from you in a dream, it could have the opposite meaning – you may soon be stripped of your authority.

If you cannot find your keys in the dream, it speaks of lost opportunities that you will deeply regret. The need to pray about this is vital.

If you have a broken key in your hand, it could mean that a promise or assurance by a senior or trusted person will not materialise.

When you see a keyhole without a key, it could mean that there will be challenges and problems amidst whatever you wish to embark on that may hinder the project.

The need to pray and fast is important.

Further reading: Matthew 16:19; Revelation 1:18

KIDNAP

Generally, this is not a good dream, and the Bible frowns upon kidnap. According to Exodus 21:16, *NIV*:

> **"Anyone who kidnaps someone is to be put to death."**

If you dream you are being kidnapped, it could mean that someone you know or trust will betray your confidence and trust and divulge your secrets to your competitors or adversaries. As Joseph says in Genesis 40:15:

> **"For indeed I was stolen away out of the land of the Hebrews."**

If you are involved in a kidnapping, it could mean that you will embarrass yourself over a matter that does not concern you.

Further reading: Deuteronomy 24:7

KILLING

This is usually a bad dream.

If you are involved in killing in the dream, you are being warned that your actions will have a destructive outcome on others.

If you are being killed, it could mean those you have helped will turn against you.

Further reading: John 10:10; Matthew 5:21; Exodus 20:13

KING

This is a positive dream.

If you see yourself before a king in the dream, it shows all your efforts and the gifts of God will bring you success and recognition.

Joseph's gift of dream interpretation brought him before the king, and eventually, he was raised to a greater height (Genesis 41:37–46).

KISSING

This dream could go either way.

If you kiss people you know in a dream, it could mean happiness and assurance of a good outcome concerning a matter. As the Scripture says in Genesis 29:13:

"when Laban heard the tidings of Jacob his sister's son, that he ran to meet him, and embraced him, and kissed him, and brought him to his house."

On the other hand, if you kiss somebody you do not know, it could be a warning of an illicit or unhealthy desire or bond being formed. As Proverbs 7:5, 13 says:

"That they may keep thee from the strange woman... So she caught him, and kissed him."

Further reading: Luke 15:20

KNIFE

"There is a generation, whose teeth are as swords, and their jaw teeth as knives, to devour the poor from off the earth, and the needy from among men" (Proverbs 30:14).

As the Scripture shows, this is a bad dream. It could mean that danger is lurking near you and the need to be careful is paramount – the enemy is closing in.

L

LABOUR

This dream could go either way.

If you see yourself labouring in a job that you are not familiar with in the dream and you are struggling, it could mean that you may experience unforeseen hardship in the future if you change your current job.

However, if you are working hard and you are calm, it could mean that you reap the rewards of your labours, as the Word of God says:

> **"For thou shalt eat the labour of thine hands: happy shalt thou be, and it shall be well with thee"** (Psalm 128:2).

LADDER

This dream could be positive or negative.

If you are climbing a ladder, it could mean that challenges before you will be overcome if you remain consistent and focused – success is before you.

If you are on top of a ladder, it shows that you will achieve your goals, and both your friends and foes will see your success.

But if you are climbing down a ladder, it could mean that you are being warned that a weakness of yours may be the cause of a downfall.

If you find yourself suddenly falling from the top of a ladder, it could mean you are being attacked by an enemy who envies you, and the need to pray is important.

Conversely, when you see a ladder in the dream, it could mean unusual improvement or unmerited favour is before you, as in the case of Jacob when he dreamt of seeing a ladder. In the course of time, he accomplished God's ordination for his life (Genesis 28:12).

LAMENTING

This dream is a mixed bag.

If in your dream state, you see people you know lamenting over you, it could mean that a trusted friend or acquaintance will disappoint or betray you. This situation will eventually turn to your advantage, as in the case of Jesus when he told his disciples not to weep and lament over him and said that their sorrow would soon be turned into joy (John 16:20). Jesus knew that although Judas would betray Him unto death, eventually He would conquer the grave and save mankind.

But when you see those you do not know lamenting, it could mean that their plots against you did not materialise. They are reaping what they have sown.

Pray that every disappointment and plan of the enemy against you shall never materialise, but they will ever turn for your good, in Jesus' Name.

LAMP

This could be a positive or negative dream.

To see a lit lamp is a good dream. It could mean that you will eventually overcome current challenges – victory will come your way.

Likewise, if you see an unlit lamp, it could mean the opposite.

LAND

Generally speaking, this dream could go either way.

To see a vast, well-cultivated area of land in a dream shows that efforts in present endeavours will be fruitful and that there will be great yield.

It could equally indicate the enlargement of your estate in the near future.

If you see uncultivated land, it could signify famine and difficulty in your life's endeavours.

LAUGHING

This dream is a mixed bag.

When you are laughing in the dream, it indicates that sudden success or wealth will come your way. You may receive an unusual blessing or visitation relating to something you have given up on. Consider the case of Sarah, who laughed because she thought all hope was lost concerning her barrenness (Genesis 18:12–13). In the course of time, God visited Sarah and she bore Isaac (Genesis 21:1–2).

If you see people you do not know looking at you and laughing, it could mean that your enemies are mocking your efforts in order to distract you from what you are determined to do.

As it says in 2 Chronicles 30:10:

> **"So the posts passed from city to city through the country of Ephraim and Manasseh even unto Zebulun: but they laughed them to scorn, and mocked them."**

LAUNDRY

Generally speaking:

When you are doing your own laundry, it shows you are cautious regarding what people think about you. You will go to great lengths to keep up good relations with people.

If you are doing someone else's laundry, it could mean that you are going out of your way to create a good impression about a friend or acquaintance, or that you are trying to cover up a secret about them.

However, if you are doing the laundry of strangers, it could mean that you are going to clean up the mess of your seniors in your workplace.

LEAKING

Usually, this is not a good dream. If you are carrying a bucket of water and it is leaking, you may be on wrong course and the efforts that you are making will not yield the desired result.

It could also mean that the effort you are putting into something is not commensurate with the reward.

LETTER

In general, receiving a letter in a dream could mean that you will get information, either positive or negative. In the Scriptures, the King of Israel received a letter from the King of Syria informing about the case of Naaman (2 Kings 5:6).

It could also mean that long-awaited good news is coming from either a close or distant connection.

When you are writing a letter in the dream, it indicates that you have an issue that you are desirous to sort out.

LIGHT

This dream is a mixed bag.

If you are in a dark environment and you suddenly see penetrative light, this is a good dream. It could mean that the fearful and thorny issues and circumstances that you are facing, which may have kept you sleepless, will be solved – possibly by divine intervention. Just as the Word of God says:

> **"Rejoice not against me, O mine enemy: when I fall, I shall arise; when I sit in darkness, the LORD shall be a light unto me"** (Micah 7:8).

If you have light all around you in the dream and the brightness begins to dim, it could mean that a threat of demonic penetration is becoming real. There is a need to pray.
  Further reading: John 12:35; Luke 11:34

Prayer Point

2 SAMUEL 21:17

Pray that the Angels of God will execute the judgment of God upon anyone or group of persons that will ever attempt to dim or quench the light of God upon your life, in Jesus' Name.

LIMOUSINE

Generally, this is a good dream. To see a limousine shows that great and magnificent opportunities and ideas are before you.

If you see yourself driving a limousine, it could mean a positive outcome in whatever you are doing.

LIMPING

This dream could go either way.

If you are limping in the dream, it could foretell an ongoing struggle. It also shows that you may go through serious challenges in life, but in the not-too-distant future, you will see the rewards of your efforts, as in the case of Jacob where he wrestled an Angel of God, and although he woke up limping, he eventually was victorious (Genesis 32:31).

On the other hand, it could mean an arrow may have been released against you.

In my own case, two of my siblings dreamt I was limping. Two days later, I began to limp physically. An audible voice told me not to take any drug, or else it would be the beginning of a problem, as it was not a physical issue but could only be dealt with spiritually. Therefore, I prayed and anointed my right hip, and the problem disappeared.

Either way, you should pray against any arrow of affliction fashioned against you, that such arrows shall ever return to their senders, in Jesus' Name.

LION

Dreaming of lions is usually negative.

When you see a lion, it is a caution to you to be sober and vigilant in your place of work, ministry, etc. You also need to be watchful and cautious in your immediate environment. As the Bible says:

> **"Be sober, be vigilant; because your adversary the devil, as a roaring lion, walketh about, seeking whom he may devour"** (1 Peter 5:8).

If you see a roaring lion, it could mean that your accusers and those fighting against you are getting frustrated and agitated about their inability to destroy you.

If you are riding a lion, you are being warned that you are taking decisions or actions that may consume you. You are playing with fire and you must be aware of the consequences.

When you see a caged lion, it could mean that a strong man or woman has been divinely caged by the Almighty.

In 2013, I dreamt of a lion at the gate of my father's compound. The same dream reoccurred a second day. In this dream, I could not get into the compound, and I climbed a tree because I was afraid of the lion. When I woke up, I called my mother, and she said that she had employed a new gateman. Three days later, the gateman was caught doing enchantment and divination using earth and throwing it at the gate.

It thus follows that the gateman was releasing curses against our family, which were symbolised in my dream as a lion. Satan is a devourer and is referred to as a lion in 1 Peter 5:8. When I realised what the man was doing, I prayed that the arrow of words he released would return back to him (Psalm 64:3).

The gateman was, of course, relieved of his duties, and seven months later, he was paralysed from the waist down.

1 PETER 5:8

Prayer Point

Bind and paralyse every spirit of lion (i.e. devouring spirit) assigned against your health, family, finances, etc., using the Name and the Blood of Jesus Christ, and return them back to their senders, in Jesus' Name.

JEREMIAH 30:16

Pray against any devouring agent assigned against you; that the Angels of God shall locate and destroy them, in Jesus' Name.

LIZARD

According to the Scriptures, this animal is referred to as unclean (Leviticus 11:30–31). Therefore, this is a negative dream.

Like any other creeping animal, it indicates a lack of enthusiasm in whatever you are doing – people will not be excited by your project.

It could also mean that you will experience slow-motion – the project will not move as fast as you want it.

LEVITICUS 11:30—31

Pray that wherever any person is using lizards or the blood of lizards to project negative aura or stagnation against you, let those manipulations be nullified by the Blood of Jesus Christ, and let them forever backfire, in Jesus' Name.

LOAD

"For the rod of the wicked shall not rest upon the lot of the righteous" (Psalm 125:3).

This is a bad dream.

If you see yourself carrying a load in the dream, it could mean that you will have problems upon problems with no solution or a difficult resolution.

It could also mean that matters before you will become a burden and will affect your wellbeing. You will never be able to finish a project that you have undertaken with this burden.

This could also signify that issues before you are being engineered by household enemies.

With such dreams, the need to make Jesus your Lord and Personal Saviour is paramount, as the Scriptures record Jesus saying:

"Come unto me, all ye that labour and are heavy laden, and I will give you rest" (Matthew 11:28).

I dreamt that a relative of mine was carrying a load, but in real life, she is successful. However, shortly after the dream, she visited me and told me that she kept having nightmares and that she was experiencing difficulty concerning her general welfare. I advised her to pray seriously. Whether she did or not, I cannot tell, but less than three months later, her husband died in a plane crash, she lost her job, and she had unusual affliction that almost destroyed her.

Further reading: 1 Kings 12:11

Prayer Point

PSALM 125:3; MATTHEW 11:28

Reject every load of the wicked that is being projected over you, your health, your endeavours, etc., and command them back to their senders. If you are going through troublesome circumstances, also pray for God's divine intervention in your life, in Jesus' Name.

LOCUSTS

To see locusts in your dream is negative and could mean that you are being faced with a devouring spirit in your life, health, business, marriage, etc.

One of the plagues the Lord sent to the Egyptians was the plague of locusts. They covered and devoured the entire land of Egypt and ate every fruit and herb, which represented everything the Egyptians had laboured for, and there was nothing left (Exodus 10:12–15). In the same vein, the enemy not only wants to project perpetual darkness against you but also to completely devour everything that concerns you.

Further reading: Joel 1:2; Revelation 9:3–5

JOEL 2:25

Bind and rebuke every spirit of locust (i.e. devouring spirit) assigned against your life, health, business, marriage, etc., and command them back to their senders, in Jesus' Name.

LOOKING

From my own perspective, when people are looking at you with concentration and without talking, it could mean that they are surprised that their plots and invocations against you have failed. Instead of you appearing before them, they have appeared before you.

It could also mean that you will overcome every opposition and stumbling block against you if you look unto Jesus. As the Scripture says:

> **"Looking unto Jesus the author and finisher of our faith"** (Hebrews 12:2).

Further reading: Matthew 14:19

LOOKING GLASS (MIRROR)

This is the main instrument used for invocation to monitor your future, business, etc.

ISAIAH 44:25; JEREMIAH 29:8

> **Pray that every satanic or demonic glasses (e.g. mirrors, crystal balls) or instruments of divination being used to monitor your star, future, business, etc., will be consumed by the Holy Ghost Fire of God. Also, pray that all those using them will run mad for your sake,** in Jesus' Name.

LOSS

See **BEREAVEMENT**

LOTTERY

See **JACKPOT**

LUGGAGE

This dream could go either way.

To see luggage in the dream could mean that you are contemplating a journey and that you are also weighing up the necessity of the visit.

On the other hand, if you lose your luggage in a dream, it could indicate that you may experience a serious setback in your current endeavour.

However, if you later find it, it means that in the long run, you will recover whatever you have lost.

M

MADNESS

According to the Scriptures, the Pharisees were filled with madness in the sense that they were furious and filled with rage against Jesus (Luke 6:11), so this is a negative dream.

If someone you know is suffering from madness, the dream reveals your state of mind about that person and the fact that you cannot understand their actions towards you.

If you are mad in the dream, it indicates those who relate to you or have contact with you have strange impressions about your actions or mannerisms.

Further reading: Daniel 4:30–33; Jeremiah 25:15–16; Deuteronomy 28:28

ISAIAH 44:25

Prayer Point

Pray that every projection of madness or foolishness against you will forever backfire unto their senders, in Jesus' Name.

MAGIC

In general, when somebody in a dream is known as a magician but in reality, he is not one, it could mean that he has links to palm reading, enchantment, invocation, or divination.

It could also indicate you are in a relationship with people possessed by the spirit of divination (Acts 16:16).

MAID

If a woman has a maid in reality and in the dream finds herself as a maid in her husband's house while the real maid becomes wife to her husband, it could mean that the maid and husband are developing a mutual lustful affection, as in Scripture in the case of Abram and Hagai, Sarah's maid (Genesis 16:3).

GENESIS 16:3

Prayer Point

Use the Name and the Blood of Jesus to bind any strange man or strange woman that may be attempting to penetrate your marriage, and pray that the Angels of God will expose and expel them, in Jesus' Name.

MAP

From my own understanding, if you are studying a map in the dream, it could mean that you are desirous of information to understand an issue.

MARK

This is a bad dream. If you see marks on your body, vehicle, property, etc., it is a clear sign that an enemy is devising an evil plot and plan. As the Word of God says:

"He has bent his bow, and set me as a mark for the arrow" (Lamentations 3:12, *NHEB*).

The mark is thus an indication of a point of contact for an attack either on your business, home, body, or marriage.

LAMENTATIONS 3:12

Prayer Point

Cancel every spiritual mark upon you or your properties for death, affliction, shame, disgrace, etc., and pray that every associated plan of the enemy against you shall backfire, in Jesus' Name.

MARKET

A market is an altar in the realm of the spirit.

"And he went... and saw others standing idle in the marketplace" (Matthew 20:3).

If you dream of a market and you are idling in it, it indicates the enemy is projecting aimlessness in your endeavours.

If the market is busy, and you are buying and selling, it indicates success in your endeavours.

Further reading: John 2:14–16; Matthew 11:16–17; Acts 16:19–23

MATTHEW 20:3; ACTS 16:19

Pray that any marketplace altar that has been erected to hinder your destiny, or to project aimlessness against you, will be consumed by the Holy Ghost Fire of God, in Jesus' Name.

MARRIAGE (WEDDING)

Dreams concerning marriages are usually tricky.

If you are single, a dream of marriage could mean you are facing future challenges getting married or settling down and you need to be more prayerful.

If you dream that different suitors are asking for your hand in marriage, it could mean that you need to be careful before you commit because not all that glitters is gold.

If you are married and you dream of marriage with someone you do not know, it could mean you need to pray against a spirit husband (incubus) or spirit wife (succubus) and pay more attention to the state of your marriage.

2 CORINTHIANS 6:14—17

Bind every spirit husband or spirit wife operating in your life. Also, use the Blood of Jesus Christ to sever every foundational link and soul tie with spirit husbands or spirit wives in your life, and separate yourself from them, in Jesus' Name.

MASQUERADE

This is a negative dream.

It could mean that your present situation or circumstance has to do with witchcraft.

If the masquerade is pursuing you, it shows those with demonic or satanic powers are after you.

If you are fighting a masquerade, it indicates that your prayer life is contending with those who are hindrances or stumbling blocks in your life.

EXODUS 22:18

Prayer Point

> **Bind and rebuke every demonic, satanic, or witchcraft power assigned against your life, destiny, marriage, business, etc,** in Jesus' Name.

MATTRESS

See **BED**

MEAT

According to the Scriptures, Peter rejected eating the meat offered to him when he was in a trance (Acts 10:12–14), so this is not a positive dream.

If you see raw meat in the dream, it shows that sacrifices have been made with or without your consent.

If you are eating raw meat, it has to do with evil covenants and initiation.

If you eat cooked meat in the dream, it speaks of spiritual pollution.

Further reading: Genesis 9:4; Exodus 12:8–9

ISAIAH 28:18; PSALM 106:28

> **If you eat meat in the dream, you need to use the Blood of Jesus Christ to cancel and separate yourself from every covenant and initiation that has been made over your life unto the powers of darkness. You should also nullify and reject every spiritual pollution in your life and body,** in Jesus' Name.

MEDICINE

This dream could be interpreted in two ways.

If you are taking medication in real life and you dream of it, it could mean the counsel, wisdom, or advice of an informed professional is necessary, relating to a matter you are contemplating.

If you are sick and you see yourself taking medicine, the end of your illness is near.

If you are giving medicine to someone and you are not a

professional, it could mean your wisdom or advice will present a solution to someone who is stressed.

Further reading: Ezekiel 47:12; Revelation 22:2; Jeremiah 46:11

MERMAID

This is a straightforward dream.

If you dream of seeing a mermaid, you are being warned that a new relationship or contact you have has a marine foundation.

If you are associating with a mermaid, it is a serious dream. It could mean that you are cohabiting with someone who has a marine foundation.

Prayer Point

2 CORINTHIANS 6:14—17

Ask God to expose and expel any man or woman in your life or in the lives of your family members that may have a marine connection or foundation; use the Name and the Blood of Jesus to draw a blood line between yourself and any person with a marine connection or foundation, in Jesus' Name.

MILLIONAIRE

This is generally a good dream.

If you see yourself as a millionaire, it could mean that your current and future efforts will have great yields or successes.

If you dream you are with millionaires, it shows your friends will be part of your success story.

JOB 22:28

Thank God for the success that He has ordained for you; decree and declare, using the Name and the Blood of Jesus, that it shall come to pass; and, bind and paralyse any power that will stand as an opposition to God's ordained success for you, in Jesus' Name.

MINISTER

According to the Word of God:

> **"men shall call you the Ministers of our God: ye shall eat the riches of the Gentiles, and in their glory shall ye boast yourselves"**
> (Isaiah 61:6),

this is a positive dream. If you see yourself as a minister, this is good. It could mean you are going to play a vital role in the lives of others – you will be a person of influence.

Further reading: Exodus 24:13, 28:35, 30:30; Ezekiel 44:11

MIRROR

See **LOOKING GLASS**

MISCARRIAGE

According to the Scripture,

"give them a miscarrying womb and dry breasts" (Hosea 9:14),

this is a bad dream.If you are not pregnant in real life and you have a miscarriage in a dream, an enemy wants to abort your current fruitful plans or ideas.

If you are pregnant in real life and you dream of a miscarriage, you need to pray against the devices of the wicked concerning your unborn child.

Prayer Point

ISAIAH 49:26

Pray that anyone who would want to abort your pregnancy or drink the blood of your unborn child, let their devices backfire; let them be drunken in their own blood, in Jesus' Name.

273

If you are barren, a dream of a miscarriage reveals to you that you are under a curse that is promoting barrenness in your life. The need to pray to cancel this is important.

Further reading: Exodus 23:26

Prayer Point

HOSEA 9:14; GALATIANS 3:13

> **Use the Name and the Blood of Jesus Christ to cancel every curse of barrenness (spiritually, physically, financially, etc.) operating in your life,** in Jesus' Name.

MONEY

This is a dream of expectation and hope.

If you are lending money to people you know, it indicates you will be a source of blessing. People will remember your good deeds.

If you are giving out money to strangers, it could also mean that you will be remembered for your good deeds. As the Scripture says:

> **"Abraham weighed to Ephron the silver, which he had named in the audience of the sons of Heth, four hundred shekels of silver, current money with the merchant"**
> (Genesis 23:16).

This could mean that some that benefit from you may want to repay your good with evil.

If you receive money from a dead person, you need to break the bond between you and that person.

Further reading: Genesis 42:25, 35; Exodus 22:7; 1 Kings 21:12; Judges 16:18; Matthew 25:18

MOON

Generally, this is a positive dream. It speaks of realisation of your goals in spite of challenges that may come your way.

It could equally indicate better times ahead spiritually. Like in the case of Joseph in Genesis 37:9:

"...behold, the sun and the moon and the eleven stars made obeisance to me."

Before I began my ministry, I dreamt of the moon. It came down to me, released three gifts, and then went back up.

Further reading: Deuteronomy 33:14

Prayer Point

DEUTERONOMY 33:14

Decree that as far as the moon endures, your blessings and good dreams will ever manifest in your life, in Jesus' Name.

MOUNTAIN

"Come ye, and let us go up to the mountain of the LORD, to the house of the God of Jacob; and he will teach us of his ways, and we will walk in his paths" (Isaiah 2:3).

When you dream of climbing a mountain, it speaks of your strength and determination to overcome issues before you. What may hinder or stop others cannot stop you.

If you are at the peak of a mountain, it could mean that you will be a role model and encourage others in similar circumstances. You will be a source of inspiration.

Further reading: Zechariah 4:7; Isaiah 25:6

MOUSE

This is a warning that the spirit of a devourer has crept into your endeavours, business, marriage, etc.

1 SAMUEL 6:4—5

Prayer Point

Bind and rebuke every spirit of mouse or rat (i.e. devouring spirits) assigned against your life, health, business, marriage, etc., and command them back to their senders, in Jesus' Name.

MOURNING

See **BEREAVEMENT**

MUSHROOM

Generally, this is a negative dream.

Mushrooms are parasites and can be harmful. This dream usually denotes a rapidly spreading infirmity like cancer.

The dream could also indicate that whatever you are doing may be unpopular.

Prayer Point

JOB 2:7

Reject every projection of infirmity and terminal illness (cancer, tumour, etc.) fashioned against you, and let them forever backfire unto their senders, in Jesus' Name.

N

NAGGING

Nagging in a dream is not good.

The Bible compares living in a desert to living with a nagging wife (Proverbs 21:19).

If you are being nagged by someone in the dream, it could mean that you are feeling oppressed or unappreciated by the person involved.

It could also show that your spirit is being vexed by the same person. You might spill your secrets to them, a decision which will hurt you in the near future as in the case of Samson and Delilah. With such nagging, she prodded him day after day so that his soul was vexed unto death. He ended up telling her all his secrets – such as where his strength lies. Hereafter, she used this against him, turning him over to his enemies (Judges 16:16–20).

If you are the one nagging, it shows that the need to open up to the person involved is vital.

Further reading: Proverbs 25:24, 27:15

NAKEDNESS

This is a negative dream because God said to Adam,

"Who told thee that thou wast naked?"
(Genesis 3:11), for God hates nakedness.

If you are naked or inappropriately dressed, uncovered, and exposed, it could mean that you are being warned of impending disgrace and scandal. As God brought humiliation to Babylon, He said:

"Thy nakedness shall be uncovered, yea, thy shame shall be seen" (Isaiah 47:3).

It could equally mean that public disgrace or scandal is coming your way in your place of work.

It could also indicate the projection of sickness, poverty, etc.

Nakedness could also signify that you are spiritually unprotected or vulnerable.

GENESIS 3:11

Bind and reject every spirit of nakedness and shame assigned against you; reject every projection and plan of shame, scandal, and exposure, and send them back to their senders, in Jesus' Name.

NAME

God gave Adam the ability to give names (Genesis 2:19–20). Therefore, man can use names for either good or destructive purposes. Being called by your name has spiritual meanings, which could either be positive or negative.

God has used the calling of names to draw one's attention to Him, as in the case of Samuel.

If you hear your name in a dream and you recognise the caller, it could mean someone desperately wants your attention.

Equally, it could mean that they are speaking about you to others who may be of help to you.

Additionally, it could mean your name is being used for invocation, enchantment, or divination.

If a dead person is calling your name, it is a serious dream that needs to be cancelled through fasting and prayers immediately.

JOHN 10:5

Prayer Point

> **Bind every strange voice that is calling your name for death, affliction, poverty, failure, etc., through invocation, enchantment, or divination; reject those calls and command those behind them to answer their own evil calls on your behalf,** in Jesus' Name.

NECKLACE

To see a new necklace in a dream could mean that you have a deepening relationship with someone. It is a signal of new affection and trust in the relationship.

It also talks about a position of authority and contains blessings if it is gold (Genesis 41:41–42).

If you are wearing a broken or an old necklace, it could signal an unfulfilled promise to a close acquaintance.

Further reading: Exodus 35:22; Numbers 31:50

NEEDLE

To dream of a needle could mean that you are being warned to be careful of an issue that you are underestimating. It is capable of destroying you if care is not taken.

Equally, it could mean you may experience inexplicable afflictions or problems.

NET

If you are the one holding a net by the river, it means that abundant blessings are coming your way (Luke 5:4–7).

However, it could also mean that there is a well-calculated plan or snare that has been set up to embarrass you.

If you find yourself covered in a net, it could mean that the enemy has set a trap for you that is about to spring into action – it will be successful if you do not pray using the Word of God:

> **"The heathen are sunk down in the pit that they made: in the net which they hid is their own foot taken"** (Psalm 9:15).

PSALM 35:7—8

Pray that anyone or group of persons who have set any net, snare, or trap against you for affliction, shame, accident, untimely death, etc., will forever fall inside of them on your behalf, in Jesus' Name.

NIPPLE (SEE BREAST)

Generally, this is a negative dream.

It speaks of lust. You are being warned of your sexual desires; temptation is before you (Ezekiel 23:3, 21).

NOISE

From my own perspective, this is not a positive dream.

If in the dream you hear a loud or odd noise in your immediate environment, it could mean you need to be wary of domestic violence.

However, if the noise is far off, it could mean that you should not get involved in a matter that does not concern you.

Further reading: Isaiah 13:4; Psalm 65:7

NUMBERS

Generally, this dream could go either way.

Seeing numbers in the dream that you remember could mean you are being told to take note of that number and relate it to your current circumstances.

But if you cannot remember the number, it could mean that there is need to reject confusion and a lack of strategy from your life.

O

OAK

According to the Bible,

"and he was strong as the oaks"
(Amos 2:9), this is a positive dream.

If you see an oak tree, it could mean that a long-term plan will be fruitful because it has a solid foundation.
Further reading: Joshua 24:26–27; Judges 6:19–21

OASIS

Oasis speaks of water in a desert. In a dream, it could signify a blessing in an unexpected place. As the Scripture says in Isaiah 43:19:

"I will do a new thing; now it shall spring forth; shall ye not know it? I will even make a way in the wilderness, and rivers in the desert."

If you dream of an oasis, it could be a sign that a new venture, although unfamiliar, will eventually flourish and have an exceptional success.
Further reading: Isaiah 35:6–7

Prayer Point

> **Thank God for blessing you and making a way for you where there seemed to be no way,** in Jesus' Name.

OATH

This is usually a negative dream. It has to do with covenant-taking or initiation.

If you see people taking an oath, it could mean you are being warned that enemies have one goal – and that is to bring you down or undo your efforts in life.

ISAIAH 8:9—10

Prayer Point

> **Use the Name and the Blood of Jesus to cancel and nullify any oath or covenant that is speaking against you. Also, command the Angels of God to locate and overthrow any person that has entered into any oath or covenant against you,** in Jesus' Name.

If you are taking an oath with people you do not know, it could mean you have unknowingly been used to carry out an act against somebody.

Further reading: Genesis 26:28; Leviticus 5:6; Joshua 9:19–20

ISAIAH 28:18

Prayer Point

Use the Blood of Jesus Christ to cancel, nullify, and separate yourself from any satanic, demonic, occultic, witchcraft, or marine oaths or covenants that you may have entered into, knowingly or unknowingly, in Jesus' Name.

OBITUARY

In general, if you see a notice announcing someone's death and the person is alive, it is a bad dream. It indicates that the spirit of death has been released against that person and the need to fast and pray to cancel it using,

"I shall not die, but live, and declare the works of the Lord" (Psalm 118:17), is important.

HOSEA 13:14; PSALM 118:17

Prayer Point

Pray vehemently against the spirit of death; use the Name and the Blood of Jesus to bind that spirit and return it back to its senders. Also, use the Word of God in Psalm 118:17 to decree that you and your beloved ones shall live and not die, in Jesus' Name.
See further prayers on BEREAVEMENT.

OCEAN

Dreams concerning oceans may indicate the following:

If the ocean is calm, it could mean that you will experience peace and tranquillity in whatever you are doing. You have good prospects and vast opportunities before you.

If you are sailing on a ship on an ocean, it could mean a happy ending in matters and situations that once frustrated you.

If the ocean is rough and stormy, it could mean that there will be serious challenges ahead. The need to have courage to face these is paramount, as in the Scriptures when Jesus rebuked the wind and the raging water to become calm (Luke 8:23–24).

Further reading: Psalm 104:6–9; Psalm 107:23–24; Job 38:8–11

OFFICE

This dream could go either way.

If you see a new, modern office before you and you love it, it speaks of new opportunities before you.

Prayer Point

REVELATION 3:8

Thank God for the new opportunities and open doors that have been set before you, in Jesus' Name.

If you are in an old office, it symbolises the important need to plan for retirement or redundancy.

When you move your chair from one office to another, it could mean a change of role but within the same environment.

As a banker, I dreamt I moved my office chair to the bullion van and the driver took it to my house.

Eventually, I started my ministry in my house and it was revealed by God that it was time for the change of office. That is why Jesus Sanctuary Ministries began from my house.

OFFICER

This dream is a mixed bag.

To see officers – either air force, military, or naval – surround your property could mean protection.

If you dream of an officer speaking to you about a matter you know nothing about, it could mean that the enemy is planning with others to hinder you.

If you dream about police officers, it symbolises witches, wizards, or occult men or women plotting against you.

EXODUS 22:18

Prayer Point

Use the Name and the Blood of Jesus to come against any association of witches, wizards, and/or occultic men or women on assignment against you. Command the Angels of God to frustrate their plans and execute God's judgment upon them, in Jesus' Name.

OIL

Anointing with oil signifies the presence of the Holy Spirit.

If you see an oil field in the dream, it symbolises vast wealth before you.

If you are purchasing oil in the dream, it could mean that your efforts to achieve in life will be successful.

If you see yourself being anointed by an evil person, it could mean that an evil spirit has been transferred to you.

If you see yourself selling oil, it could mean that you should be conscious of not making a wrong decision about a serious matter.

OLD MAN OR WOMAN

If you see an old man or woman in a dream, it could mean you need the counsel or input of an experienced person about a particular issue. According to the Scriptures, King Rehoboam rejected the counsel of the elders and took advice from the young men he grew up with, which caused the division of his kingdom (2 Chronicles 10:8–16).

OPERATION

Dreams concerning operations are not usually good.

If you are healthy in real life and you dream you are undergoing an operation, it could mean you need to watch your wellbeing. Your life could be affected if care is not taken.

EXODUS 15:26

Prayer Point

Besides physically watching your wellbeing, also pray against any projection of infirmity or affliction; use the Name and the Blood of Jesus to reject them and return them back to their senders, in Jesus' Name.

On the other hand, if you are in hospital and you dream of an operation, it could mean that it will be successful if you pray very well.

1 PETER 2:24

Prayer Point

Thank God and decree by the Name and the Blood of Jesus, using the Word of God in 1 Peter 2:24, that total healing and recovery will forever be your portion, in Jesus' Name.

ORANGE (COLOUR)

If you are wearing orange in a dream, it could mean that you have been spiritually condemned and only fasting and prayer can deliver you.

ISAIAH 54:17; ISAIAH 10:1

Prayer Point

Pray seriously to cancel and nullify any satanic judgment or condemnation that has been passed against you; reject them and decree that they will ever return them back to their senders, in Jesus' Name.

ORANGE (FRUIT)

To see a tree with oranges speaks of a fruitful and enduring relationship.

ORCHARD

This is a very good dream. It could mean that your efforts and endeavours in life will yield fruit and that you will face little challenge.

Prayer Point

GENESIS 49:22

Bless the name of God for causing you to yield fruit, and for allowing your endeavours to be successful, in Jesus' Name.

OUIJA BOARD

This is a bad dream. It speaks of the spirit of manipulation. It could mean that the person is trying to use an Ouija board as an altar to make you do things you would not ordinarily do.

The need to pray using,

> **"Surely there is no enchantment against Jacob, neither is there any divination against Israel"** (Numbers 23:23), is important.

NUMBERS 23:23

Prayer Point

Use the Name of Jesus to command the Angels of God to locate and frustrate all those that are manipulating you, your destiny, your finances, your education, etc.; decree that they will never live to execute their plans, in Jesus' Name.

DEUTERONOMY 18:10

Prayer Point

Command the Angels of God to execute God's judgment upon all those that are monitoring you, your family, education, star, business, etc., for evil, in Jesus' Name.

OVATION

Generally speaking, if people you know are applauding you in a dream, it is good – it indicates that you did not betray trust concerning a controversial issue.

However, if the ovation is largely from people you do not know, it could mean that a decision could have an unexpected result.

OWL

According to the Scriptures, owls connote negativity:

> **"the owl also and the raven shall dwell in it: and he shall stretch out upon it the line of confusion, and the stones of emptiness"** (Isaiah 34:11).

This is naturally not a good dream. Owls, like all night birds, could symbolise an enemy or adversary planning a serious setback or attack.

Further reading: Leviticus 11:13, 16

ISAIAH 8:10; JOB 5:12

Prayer Point

Pray that the plans of any adversary or enemy concerning you shall backfire, and command the Angels of God to frustrate their plots and plans, in Jesus' Name.

OX

An ox in the dream represents strength as in the Word of God:

> **"but much increase is by the strength of the ox"** (Proverbs 14:4).

It equally indicates a prosperous future, in your business, marriage, and other relationships.

Further reading: Psalm 144:14

P

PAIN

As the psalmist said:

"Fear took hold upon them there, and pain, as of a woman in travail" (Psalm 48:6).

This dream is negative.

Pain all over your body in a dream indicates that the enemy is trying to afflict you in matters concerning your general wellbeing, including your physical health, business transactions, and relationships.

A dream of pain in a specific part of the body indicates that it is under attack and, if adequate prayer is not applied, it could lead to other terminal diseases. The wicked ones may have used an effigy to fight you.

If an internal organ is in pain, the enemy may have used an image to fight you, as in the Scriptures:

"For the king of Babylon stood at the parting of the way, at the head of the two ways, to use divination: he made his arrows bright, he consulted with images, he looked in the liver" (Ezekiel 21:21).

ISAIAH 54:17; PSALM 37:14—15

Return every arrow of affliction, sickness, accident, death, etc., fashioned against you back to their senders, in Jesus' Name.

EZEKIEL 21:21

Pray that anyone who is using your image to release affliction against any part or organ of your body, let their projections forever backfire unto their own bodies, in Jesus' Name.

PAINT

As Jeremiah pointed out:

> "though thou rentest thy face with painting, in vain shalt thou make thyself fair; thy lovers will despise thee, they will seek thy life" (Jeremiah 4:30).

This dream is not positive.

If you dream of seeing someone you know painting, it could mean that they are not giving you a true picture of a matter between the two of you.

On the other hand, if you are the one painting, it could

mean that there are issues that you yourself are not giving the true picture of.

PALACE

According to the Scriptures:

> **"At the end of twelve months he walked in the palace of the kingdom of Babylon. The king spake, and said, Is not this great Babylon, that I have built for the house of the kingdom by the might of my power, and for the honour of my majesty?"**
> (Daniel 4:29–30).

Typically, this dream is positive.

To see a palace in the dream could represent the unusual expansion of whatever you are doing and abundance in the latter years of your life.

Furthermore, it could also mean that your hard work will be fruitful.

Further reading: 1 Kings 7:1–7

JOB 42:12; JOB 22:28

Prayer Point

Thank God for blessing you with abundance and fruitfulness. Decree that your latter end will ever be greater than your beginning, all the days of your life, in Jesus' Name.

PALM TREE

This is usually a good dream. A palm tree signifies that enduring effort will cause your endeavours to blossom and to be fruitful. You shall eat the fruit of your labour and be a blessing unto others, as the psalmist likens the righteous to flourishing like a palm tree (Psalm 92:12).

Further reading: Leviticus 23:40–42

Prayer Point

PSALM 92:12

> **Decree that, according to the will of God, you will flourish, be fruitful, and blossom in all your endeavours,** in Jesus' Name.

PARCEL

From my counselling experience, to send or receive a parcel in a dream is an indication that you may have a pleasant surprise. This may be from a close acquaintance or else from someone that you least expect or think that has forgotten you.

PARTNERSHIP

By and large, when you are in partnership with someone in real life but do not see them as your associate in the dream, it could mean that the relationship will not last – there may be future trouble.

2 CORINTHIANS 6:14

Use the Blood of Jesus to cancel and separate yourself from any association, friendship, acquaintance, or partnership that is not of God, in Jesus' Name.

PASSENGER

In general, when you dream of being a passenger on a journey, it could mean that you are not playing an effective role in your present occupation. The decisions of others are likely to affect the outcome of your efforts and transactions.

PASSPORT

From my counselling experience, this dream usually relates to a decision you are about to take.

If you see a clean passport in the dream, it could mean that investigations concerning your issue will be in your favour.

If you see that your passport is covered, it could mean that you won't have the opportunity to influence others in affairs that you will be involved in.

If you see that your passport is squeezed and old, it shows that there may be a negative outcome of an investigation involving you. The need to be prayerful is very important.

If you find that your passport is missing, it could mean that you will have serious setbacks.

PASSWORD

Generally, if you cannot remember your password in the dream, this could indicate that you may face an embarrassing situation as a result of your own carelessness.

Prayer Point

PSALM 109:29

Use the Name and the Blood of Jesus to bind every spirit of shame and disgrace that has been sent on assignment against you; command them to return to their senders, in Jesus' Name.

PASTURES

As the Word of God says:

> **"He maketh me to lie down in green pastures"** (Psalm 23:2).

And:

> **"I will feed them in a good pasture"** (Ezekiel 34:14).

Green pastures in a dream are good. Typically, they represent an abundance of provision. They suggest that you will never suffer lack and that your efforts in life will move from strength to strength.

In the case of one who is newly married, this may also signify that your marital relationship will be fruitful and enduring.

PSALM 23:2

Thank God for removing lack from your life and decree that the abundance and fruitfulness that God has planned for you must come into manifestation, in Jesus' Name.

PAVEMENT

Generally speaking, to dream about a pavement represents moving forward.

If the pavement looks good and clean, it could signify that you will not have hindrances or challenges moving forward.

If the pavement is dark, this represents a vital need to be careful and patient in where you are going.

PENIS

See **GENITALS**

PENNY

See **COINS**

PERFUME

In most cases, a dream of perfume has to do with your impression of, or feelings towards, a person.

If you are a man and you dream of receiving a gift of perfume from a woman in the dream, it could mean she has made a lasting impression on you. It could also signal a sudden interest on the part of the woman.

However, if you are a woman and you receive a gift of perfume from a man in a dream, it does not tell much of his heart towards you – it talks more of a gesture of casual interest.

Perfume exchanged between a husband and wife in a dream could signify a statement of expectation and mutual respect between them.

Further reading: Exodus 30:35; John 12:3; Mark 14:3

EZEKIEL 8:11; JEREMIAH 18:17

Prayer Point

At times, use the Name and the Blood of Jesus to cancel any strange aura or atmosphere that has been projected into your life, and command the East wind to return them back to their senders, in Jesus' Name.

PHOTOGRAPH (SEE PICTURES)

In general, when your photograph is being taken in a dream it indicates that your decisions or actions will attract attention, either positively or negatively.

Images were used in idolatrous worship. Therefore, someone's picture being taken could mean an evil altar is being set up to afflict you. The Scripture forbids such altars:

"Thou shalt not make unto thee any graven image, or any likeness of any thing that is in heaven above, or that is in the earth beneath, or that is in the water under the earth" (Exodus 20:4).

Further reading: Romans 1:23
Prayer: See prayers on PICTURES.

PHYSICIAN

See **DOCTOR**

PICTURES

Pictures in the dream have different stories to tell.

If you find yourself looking at a picture of your younger self, this could show that you are being critical of your present self and/or physical appearance.

When you see people holding your picture and you do not know them, there is a need for you to watch out for unsubstantiated criticism directed towards you.

Equally, this could indicate that your picture is being used in an evil altar for spiritual manipulation. You need to pray against this. As Moses said in the Scriptures:

"and destroy all their pictures, and destroy all their molten images, and quite pluck down all their high places" (Numbers 33:52).

EZEKIEL 21:21; NUMBERS 23:23

Pray that all those that are using your picture for enchantment, divination, or invocation will never live to execute their plans; their enchantment, divination, and invocation shall ever return back unto them, in Jesus' Name.

DEUTERONOMY 7:5

Wherever anyone has taken your picture to any shrine, altar, coven, or temple for evil, or set up an image to represent you for evil manipulations, let the Holy Ghost Fire of God destroy those altars and images, and let the Angels of God locate those involved for judgment, in Jesus' Name.

PIG (SWINE)

This animal is categorised as unclean in the Bible (Leviticus 11:7–8). Therefore, to dream of a pig is not a positive omen. It could mean that you are associating with those who have unclean spirits.

Furthermore, it could also mean that there are new contacts or connections in your life that are not right.

Further Reading: Deuteronomy 14:8; Matthew 7:6

DEUTERONOMY 14:8; MATTHEW 18:18

Prayer Point

Use the Name and the Blood of Jesus to bind and paralyse any unclean spirit that may be operating in your life or in your foundation, in Jesus' Name.

2 CORINTHIANS 6:14—17

Prayer Point

Use the Blood of Jesus to separate yourself from all those in your life that may be possessed with an unclean spirit, in Jesus' Name.

PIGEON

See **BIRD**

PIT

See **HOLE**

PLATFORM

If you dream of a platform, this generally speaks of a new level of recognition and fame in your current endeavour.

NEHEMIAH 8:5; PSALM 23:5

Prayer Point

Thank God for taking you to new heights in your endeavours. Also, pray that all those that do not want you to ascend to those heights will never live to execute their plans, in Jesus' Name.

PLEADING

As Job said:

"Hear now my reasoning, and hearken to the pleadings of my lips" (Job 13:6), so this dream could go either way.

When you see yourself pleading in a dream, it could mean that you are convinced about an issue, and if necessary, you will go to any lengths to make your case.

However, if somebody else is pleading with you, the need to weigh options before you make any decision is important.

Further reading: 1 Samuel 24:15

POISON

Poison in a dream is negative.

If you see another person taking poison, it shows that you have negatively influenced their decision. He or she is reacting to the way and manner that you presented the matter.

If you dream of mistakenly taking poison, it could mean that you are being warned that your attitude or behaviour towards a close acquaintance is being manipulated from stories that you may have heard (i.e., you are reacting to them based on false information).

2 SAMUEL 15:34

Pray that the Angels of God will frustrate and overthrow all those that are manipulating you for evil, in Jesus' Name.

On the other hand, this dream could be interpreted literally.

In 2010, I had a dream that a fellow pastor invited me to a dinner, but he wanted to poison me. Early the next morning, the same pastor called me and said that he was arranging a surprise dinner with five other pastors for his wife's birthday on Saturday evening. I asked him to send me his address.

Even though I did not attend the party, the pastor, even to this day, did not ask me why I did not turn up. The pastor sounded nice, but his tongue was full of poison, as the Word of God says:

"But the tongue can no man tame; it is an unruly evil, full of deadly poison" (James 3:8).

2 KINGS 4:40; PROVERBS 21:18

Pray that all those that are secretly plotting to poison you will never live to execute their plans; let them become a ransom for yourself, in Jesus' Name.

POLICE

Generally, police in the dream represent friends or relations unexpectedly ganging up against you.

It may also symbolise witches, wizards, or occult men or women plotting against you.

ISAIAH 8:9—10

Use the Name of Jesus to command the Angels of God to locate and scatter any gang-up or association of household enemies, witches, or wizards against you, in Jesus' Name.

POOL

This dream could either be positive or negative.

When you see a full swimming pool in the dream, this indicates happy occasions and events ahead of you.

A dry pool speaks of emptiness and difficult situations and circumstances.

ISAIAH 43:19

Cancel and nullify any projection of dryness and emptiness that the enemy has set against you. Also, decree that every difficult situation in your life will turn around for your good, in Jesus' Name.

A dirty and unkempt pool could mean an unhappy ending concerning your general wellbeing.

POT

This dream has several mixed interpretations.

If in the dream, you see full pots, this speaks of the fulfilment of your heart's desires, as when Jesus performed his first miracle and He told the people to fill water pots to the brim and turned the water into wine (John 2:7–12).

Likewise, if you see an empty pot, it could symbolise that your efforts over an issue will not be fulfilling.

If you find yourself carrying a pot in the dream, this is negative – it signifies those under a curse of hardship and poverty.

If you see a boiling pot, this is also negative – you may not profit from a business or transaction, like when God asked Jeremiah:

> **"What seest thou? And I said, I see a seething pot; and the face thereof is toward the north. Then the LORD said unto me, Out of the north an evil shall break forth upon all the inhabitants of the land"**
> (Jeremiah 1:13–14).

JEREMIAH 1:13—14

Pray that every evil pot harbouring your name, pictures, hair, etc., or holding your blessings, will be destroyed by the Holy Ghost Fire of God, in Jesus' Name.

GALATIANS 3:13

Use the Name and the Blood of Jesus to nullify and separate yourself from any curse of hardship that may be operating in your life and your foundation, in Jesus' Name.

PRAISE

According to the Word of God:

> **"in the spirit, and not in the letter; whose praise is not of men, but of God"**
> (Romans 2:29).

This dream could go either way.

If somebody who you know is praising you before others, you need to be careful of the counsel you receive from them.

However, when somebody who you do not know is praising you, this indicates that there is a need to help those around you who are less privileged than yourself.

PRECIPICE

Generally, when you find yourself on a precipice (i.e. a steep cliff), it is a dire warning that you must retrace your steps regarding a decision or project that you have embarked on, irrespective of how far you have gone or how painful the process may be.

PREGNANCY

Dreams about pregnancy are interesting.

As a woman, to be pregnant in a dream could represent the fulfilment of a long-awaited desire.

PROVERBS 23:18; PSALM 145:19

Prayer Point

Thank God for the manifestation of your long-awaited expectations and desires, in Jesus' Name.

It could also indicate a renewed intimacy and bond in a relationship that will bring forth good fruits in the near future. In the Scriptures it says:

> **"And Isaac intreated the LORD for his wife, because she was barren: and the LORD was intreated of him, and Rebekah his wife conceived"** (Genesis 25:21).

She brought forth two nations.

When you are barren in real life and you dream of being pregnant, you need to pray against those monitoring you who prevent you from being fruitful, for the Word of God says:

"And ye shall serve the LORD your God... There shall nothing cast their young, nor be barren, in thy land" (Exodus 23:25–26).

Further reading: Hosea 9:14

PSALM 113:9

Prayer Point

Use the Name and the Blood of Jesus to bind and paralyse every spirit of barrenness on assignment against you; command them back to their senders, in Jesus' Name.

ISAIAH 44:25

Prayer Point

Pray that all those monitoring you or fighting your fruitfulness will never live to execute their plans, in Jesus' Name.

PRISON

See **JAIL**

PROSTITUTE (HARLOT, WHORE)

If you see a prostitute, it is a bad dream. It could mean that you must guard yourself against unfamiliar associations – you are being warned of spiritual pollution, for the Word of God says:

> **"Do you not know that he who unites himself with a prostitute is one with her in body? For it is said, 'The two will become one flesh'"** (1 Corinthians 6:16, *NIV*).

Also, you must be mindful of a confidant who may expose your secret for monetary or selfish reasons, as in the Scriptures:

> **"he that keepeth company with harlots spendeth his substance"** (Proverbs 29:3).

Further reading: Leviticus 19:29; Genesis 38:15; Proverbs 7:10; Joshua 2:1–13

PULPIT (PODIUM)

Generally speaking, this speaks of a platform and a position of authority and influence, either spiritually or otherwise. As in the Scriptures:

"And Ezra the scribe stood upon a pulpit of wood, which they had made for the purpose… And Ezra opened the book in the sight of all the people; (for he was above all the people;) and when he opened it, all the people stood up" (Nehemiah 8:4–5).

MATTHEW 22:14; JAMES 4:6

Prayer Point

Thank God for His calling upon your life and for placing you in a position of authority and influence; ask for the grace to carry out this mantle, in Jesus' Name.

PURPLE

Usually, this colour signifies royalty – a position of rank, honour, dominion, and authority.

The colour also connotes wealth, prosperity, and luxury. According to the Scriptures:

"And Mordecai went out from the presence of the king in royal apparel of blue and white, and with a great crown of gold, and with a garment of fine linen and purple: and the city of Shushan rejoiced and was glad" (Esther 8:15).

Further reading: Exodus 28:4–5; Luke 16:9; Revelation 18:12

Prayer Point

ESTHER 8:15

Thank God for giving you dominion and for giving you authority. Also, thank God for the wealth, prosperity, and financial blessings that He has ordained for you and decree that this ordination for your life must come into manifestation, in Jesus' Name.

PYTHON (SPIRIT OF DIVINATION)

From my counselling experience, this is not a good dream – the spirits of deception and divination are involved (Acts 16:16). You must be wary of your associates, their counsel, and their advice.

More circumspectly, you must be wary of the counsel that you are taking over a matter or situation you are contemplating.

Prayer Point

ACTS 16:16; NUMBERS 23:23

Use the Name and the Blood of Jesus to bind and paralyse every spirit of divination that has been set against you, in Jesus' Name.

DEUTERONOMY 18:10

Pray that all those that are using divination against you will never live to execute their plans, but let the Angels of God locate them for judgment, in Jesus' Name.

Q

QUARREL (CONTENTION)

According to the Scriptures:

> "For John had said unto Herod, It is not lawful for thee to have thy brother's wife. Therefore Herodias had a quarrel against him, and would have killed him; but she could not" (Mark 6:18–19).

If you are quarrelling with people in the dream, it could mean that you are not comfortable with some things among your close associates.

If somebody is quarrelling with you without any reason, it shows that your current successes are not going down well with others.

Further reading: Proverbs 17:14; 15:18; Acts 15:37–39

Prayer Point

ISAIAH 49:25

Pray that God will release His Angels to contend with all those that are contending with you; those contending with you will never live to execute their plans, in Jesus' Name.

QUANTITY

Generally, if you see a large quantity of something in the dream, it could mean that you are being cautioned not to be overwhelmed. You should remain calm, irrespective of whatever is coming your way.

QUESTIONING

This is not usually a good dream, according to the Scriptures. David (Psalm 10:1) and Habakkuk (Habakkuk 1:2) questioned God because they were frustrated and burdened with troubles.

If you are questioning certain things in a dream, it could mean that you want to be convinced about something that has big prospects but of which you are not sure.

However, if others are questioning, be ready for difficulty and doubt over the outcome.

R

RABBIT (HARE)

As the Scriptures categorised this animal as unclean (Leviticus 11:6), this is a negative dream.

To dream of a rabbit in your house generally speaks of household devourers with an element of witchcraft infiltration in your home, business, etc.

MATTHEW 18:18

Prayer Point

Use the Name and the Blood of Jesus to bind and paralyse any witchcraft infiltration or devouring spirit operating against you and in your household, in Jesus' Name.

RAG

See **TATTERED CLOTHING**

RAGE (ANGER, WRATH)

The Bible tells us to put off all these (rage, anger, wrath) out of your mouth (Colossians 3:8). To rage in the dream is a negative signal. It shows that you need to be in control of a matter or situation and that you should not allow your pride to get the better of you.

319

You are being warned that your temper may affect opportunities before you, as King Solomon said:

"A man of great wrath shall suffer punishment" (Proverbs 19:19).

Further reading: Proverbs 14:29

PROVERBS 14:29, PROVERBS 19:19

Prayer Point

Ask God for the grace to overcome the spirits of rage and anger, and to not allow them to hinder you possessing your possessions or making the most of the opportunities that have been set before you, in Jesus' Name.

RAIN

In most instances, soft, drizzly rain suggests blessings. According to the Scriptures:

"Be glad then, ye children of Zion, and rejoice in the LORD your God: for he hath given you the former rain moderately, and he will cause to come down for you the rain, the former rain, and the latter rain in the first month" (Joel 2:23).

320

Unlike downpours, light rain symbolises that your efforts and dedication are not easily hindered – only heavy rain can stop or impede you, like the heavy rain God caused that consumed every living thing except for Noah and his livestock (Genesis 17–24).

JOEL 2:23

Prayer Point

Thank God for blessing you and for releasing showers of blessings over your lives, in Jesus' Name.

RAINBOW

According to the Scriptures, the rainbow was a sign of the everlasting covenant between God and Noah. It signified that God would never again destroy the earth by the waters of the flood (Genesis 9:11–16). This is a dream of assurance that your desires and expectations will come to pass in spite of current circumstances.

PROVERBS 23:18, GENESIS 9:11—16

Prayer Point

Thank God because His word and covenant over your life must surely come to pass, and that despite the current circumstances and situation you may be going through, He will fulfil your hearts desires, in Jesus' Name.

RAPE

According to the Word of God:

"But if a man find a betrothed damsel in the field, and the man force her, and lie with her: then the man only that lay with her shall die" (Deuteronomy 22:25).

This is obviously not a good dream. If you are a single woman and you dream of being raped by someone that you know, it signifies that his feelings towards you are lustful.

However, if a stranger is raping you, it could mean that a new relationship will not be genuine.

If a man dreams of raping a woman, it could mean that a relationship he is forming will be problematic and may destroy his reputation.

Further reading: 2 Samuel 13:12, 14

2 SAMUEL 13:12; PSALM 109:29

Prayer Point

Use the Name and Blood of Jesus to decree and declare that any projection of scandal against you will forever fail and backfire, in Jesus' Name.

RAT (MOUSE)

From my counselling experience, to dream of a rat is not

good, as it speaks of a household devourer. The Scriptures say:

> **"They that sanctify themselves, and purify themselves... and the abomination, and the mouse, shall be consumed together, saith the LORD"** (Isaiah 66:17).

Therefore, there are those around you who do not add any value and there is need to pray against them.

Further reading: 1 Samuel 6:45

Prayer: See prayers on MOUSE.

RAZOR

A razor is a secret, destructive instrument in the realm of the spirit.

To dream of somebody with a razor trying to attack you is a clear indication of wicked hostility towards your actions – just as Delilah used a razor as an instrument to destroy the strength of Samson (Judges 16:17–19).

Further reading: Numbers 6:5; Psalm 52:2

Prayer Point

ISAIAH 54:17

Pray that any weapon formed or fashioned against you by wicked men or women to destroy you, or to remove your source of strength, has failed, and those weapons have backfired upon their senders, in Jesus' Name.

RED

See **COLOUR**

REJECTION

According to the Scriptures, God said unto Samuel:

> **"for they have not rejected thee, but they have rejected me, that I should not reign over them"** (1 Samuel 8:7).

This dream could be either positive or negative.

If you dream that close acquaintances are rejecting you, this could mean that you need to change your ways with regard to people you have known for a long time.

1 SAMUEL 8:7

Prayer Point

> **Bind, paralyse, and reject every spirit of rejection or hatred that the enemy has projected against you and your family, and return them back to their senders,** in Jesus' Name.

However, if in the dream you see other people rejecting you and you are not worried, it could mean that a healthy separation process is going on in your life.

2 CORINTHIANS 6:14

Pray that God will separate you from all those in your life that are not of God, in Jesus' Name.

RESIGNATION

In general, if you are a working person and you dream that you resign from your job, this could mean that the enemy wants to frustrate you.

MATTHEW 18:18

Bind, paralyse, and rebuke every spirit of frustration that has been sent on assignment against you, in Jesus' Name.

RESTING

Such a dream could be a warning that you are overworking yourself – the need to get some rest is paramount, for the Word of God says:

> **"And my people shall dwell in a peaceable habitation, and in sure dwellings, and in quiet resting places"** (Isaiah 32:18).

REVENGE

This is a negative dream.

When dreaming of taking revenge, it could indicate that you regret past actions over something still troubling you.

It could also mean that you have an unforgiving spirit and there is a need to deal with it.

MATTHEW 6:12

Prayer Point

Pray that God will remove every unforgiving spirit from your life, and that He will give you a forgiving spirit instead, in Jesus' Name.

However, if you see someone else taking revenge on you, it could mean that somebody who you offended is pretending to be on good terms with you. However, they will retaliate much later. As the Word of God says:

"Because the Philistines have dealt by revenge, and have taken vengeance with a despiteful heart, to destroy it for the old hatred" (Ezekiel 25:15).

PSALM 59:2—3

Prayer Point

Ask God to expose and expel any secret enemy in your life that is seeking a way to attack; let the ever Angels of God frustrate and judge them, in Jesus' Name.

RIDING

The interpretation of this dream depends on the animal you are riding.

If you dream you are riding a horse, it could mean that you will have resounding success in your business and life's endeavours, just as Elijah was gloriously carried in the chariot of horses to Heaven (2 Kings 2:11).

But if you are riding a donkey in the dream, it symbolises that your efforts in life will not only be sluggish but also unfavourable.

Prayer Point

ISAIAH 8:10

Cancel and nullify any projection or efforts by the enemy to cause your efforts to be sluggish and unfavourable; decree that such projections will ever return back to their senders, in Jesus' Name.

RIVER

There are several possible interpretations for a river in the dream.

If you find yourself swimming in a river with strangers, this may indicate that you have close relationships or contacts with marine connections.

If you find yourself living in the river, having cars, properties, etc., this speaks of you having a link to a marine spirit. The need for deliverance is important.

To bathe in a river is a negative dream. It shows that you may have been covenanted to the powers in the water, either as a child or an adult.

2 CORINTHIANS 6:14—17

Prayer Point

> **Use the Name and the Blood of Jesus to separate yourself from any marine connection that you may have, whether it be through your foundation, through being covenanted to the powers in the water or being possessed by a marine spirit, or through your relationships,** in Jesus' Name.

If you are on a boat in a calm river, this could signify overcoming your challenges before you – God has a pleasant future in store for you.

REVELATION 12:11

Prayer Point

> **Thank God for giving you the grace to overcome the challenges that have been or will ever be placed before you,** in Jesus' Name.

On the other hand, if you find that you are on a boat in a boisterous and turbulent river, this signifies the opposite, as when Jesus and his disciples were on a boat in a turbulent sea, which was not calm until He rebuked the wind and sea (Luke 8:22–24).

If you dream of walking along a riverbank, it could mean that you will have a pleasurable relationship.

ROAD

This dream could either be positive or negative.

When you see a tarred, broad road in the dream, it could mean that you will have difficulties that you will overcome – a road that is tarred is better than a road that is not.

But if you see an unkempt road that is not tarred, it could mean that you will face serious hindrances and impediments. You may reach your goal eventually, but it will be time-consuming and will require conscientious efforts.

ISAIAH 45:2; MATTHEW 15:13

Prayer Point

Use the Name and the Blood of Jesus to pray against anything that the enemy has set before you as an obstruction and to hinder you from actualising what God has ordained for you; let them be uprooted by the Angels of God, in Jesus' Name.

If you find yourself before two tarred roads in the dream, a lonely road is better than a busy one. A busy road teeming with all sorts of characters indicates a path that may not lead you to a successful end, spiritually speaking.

On the other hand, a lonely road indicates a path that may eventually lead to a righteous and successful ending, for the Word of God says:

> **"Enter through the narrow gate. For wide is the gate and broad is the road that leads to destruction, and many enter through it. But small is the gate and narrow the road that leads to life, and only a few find it"**
> (Matthew 7:13–14, *NIV*).

MATTHEW 7:13—14

Prayer Point

Ask God to grant you the grace to walk down the path that He has ordained for you, which will lead you to a glorious end, in Jesus' Name.

ROADBLOCK

As the Word of God says,

> **"There shall not any man be able to stand before thee all the days of thy life"**
> (Joshua 1:5),

a roadblock of any kind in a dream is not good. It shows a deliberate attempt by the wicked ones to stop you by any means possible.

JOSHUA 1:5

Bind and paralyse every spirit of frustration on assignment against you, your family, your business, your education, etc, in Jesus' Name.

PROVERBS 21:18

Decree that all those that are projecting frustration against you will never live to execute their plans, and command the projections back to their senders, in Jesus' Name.

ROCK

This speaks of solidity, strength, resilience, and protection, as the psalmist proclaimed:

> **"The LORD is my rock, and my fortress, and my deliverer; my God, my strength"**
> (Psalm 18:2).

If you see rocks around you, this signifies protection.

If you are on top of a rock, this symbolises that you are on a solid foundation. According to the Word of God, the house built by a man on a rock was not shaken by storms and flood because it was built on a solid foundation (Luke 6:48).

Thank God for His divine protection and solid foundation over your life and family, in Jesus' Name.

If you see yourself climbing a rock, this could signify that although difficult challenges may be ahead of you, if you persist, it will be worthwhile.

However, if you find yourself on a rock and falling, this could mean serious judgment, as the Word of God says:

"And a stone of stumbling, and a rock of offence, even to them which stumble at the word, being disobedient: whereunto also they were appointed" (1 Peter 2:8).

1 PETER 2:8

Cancel and nullify any satanic judgment and condemnation that has been passed over your life, in Jesus' Name.

ROOF

According to the Scriptures,

"they uncovered the roof where he was: and when they had broken it up" (Mark 2:4), a house without a roof in a dream symbolises exposure and warns of calamity and impending doom upon a household.

Further reading: 2 Samuel 11:2

MARK 2:4

Pray that all those trying to expose you and your family members for shame, and in order to cause calamity in your family, will never live to execute their plans; let their evil plans and desire forever backfire, in Jesus' Name.

ROOM

See **BEDROOM**

ROOT

According to the Scriptures:

> **"Say thou, Thus saith the Lord GOD; Shall it prosper? shall he not pull up the roots thereof, and cut off the fruit thereof, that it wither? it shall wither in all the leaves of her spring, even without great power or many people to pluck it up by the roots thereof"** (Ezekiel 17:9).

A root signifies an origin. When you see a tree root in a dream and the tree itself is dry, it could mean that issues you

333

are facing, which may be causing you sleepless nights, have to do with past relationships, connections, or foundations.

PSALM 11:3; HEBREWS 12:29

Use the Name of Jesus to command the Holy Ghost Fire of God to locate and destroy anything in your foundation not of God, acting in opposition to what God has ordained for you, in Jesus' Name.

ROPE

According to the Scriptures:

> **"[Samson] said unto her, If they bind me fast with new ropes that never were occupied, then shall I be weak, and be as another man. Delilah therefore took new ropes, and bound him therewith"** (Judges 16:11–12).

Therefore, this dream is negative.

When you see yourself tied with a rope in a dream, it symbolises that the source of your problems is complicated and the need to face them with great seriousness and tact is important.

MATTHEW 12:29; MATTHEW 18:18

> **Anywhere the evil ones have tied your blessings, your fruitfulness, your destiny, etc., command the Holy Ghost Fire of God to locate and destroy those ropes, and command your blessings to be released unto you,** in Jesus' Name.

However, if you just see a rope, it is a warning that enemies are conspiring to hinder you.

ISAIAH 8:9—10

> **Pray that all those that are plotting and conspiring to hinder you, your destiny, your blessings, your finances, etc., will never live to execute their plans; command the Angels of God to frustrate and scatter them, and the judgment of God to come upon them,** in Jesus' Name.

ROUNDABOUT (CIRCLE)

From my own perspective, a roundabout is an altar — as is everything in circle-form, because the Scriptures say:

> **"So the ark of the LORD compassed the city, going about it once: and they came into the camp, and lodged in the camp"** (Joshua 6:11).

When you dream of a roundabout, it could mean that your enemies and adversaries are trying to enforce limitations on whatever you are doing by the power of enchantment and divination.

It could equally indicate that people around you are against what you are doing.

Further reading: Isaiah 40:22

ISAIAH 40:22

Prayer Point

Command the Holy Ghost Fire of God to locate and destroy altars that have been erected at any roundabout, which the enemy is using to fight and hinder you, in Jesus' Name.

JEREMIAH 3:22

Prayer Point

Bind and reject any projection of rising and falling that has been released against you, and use the Name and the Blood of Jesus to return such projections back to their senders, in Jesus' Name.

RUBBISH

See **GARBAGE**

RUNNING

According to the Scriptures:

> **"And the watchman saw another man running: and the watchman called unto the porter, and said, Behold another man running alone. And the king said, He also bringeth tidings"** (2 Samuel 18:26).

In general, when you see yourself running without being chased, it could mean that you have a secret desire you are pursuing at all costs. If care is not taken, the pursuit may consume you.

On the other hand, if you are running away from pursuers, it could mean that competitors are trying to stop you or overpower you, but their efforts will be in vain.

Further reading: 2 Kings 5:24

Prayer Point

EXODUS 14:13—14

Command the Angels of God to frustrate and overthrow every stubborn pursuer after your destiny, in Jesus' Name.

S

SACK (BAG)

If you dream of looking at a sack that appears to be full, it indicates an unexpected pleasant gift from an unlikely source. In the Bible, Joseph's brothers fortunately received gifts from him, saying:

> **"Fill the men's sacks with food, as much as they can carry, and put every man's money in his sack's mouth"** (Genesis 44:1).

SACK (LETTER OF TERMINATION)

Generally, if you receive the sack in the dream, it could indicate unexpected decisions or events in your place of work or another situation.

One of my church members dreamt she received a letter of termination, but she forgot to pray about it. Some months later during a reorganisation, her employers were asked to make a list of those whose jobs could be cut, and her name was included.

If she had taken the dream seriously and prayed and fasted, she would have benefitted and remained in her workplace.

SACRIFICE

According to the Bible:

"And they made a calf in those days, and offered sacrifice unto the idol, and rejoiced in the works of their own hands" (Acts 7:41).

This is a negative dream.

If you dream of a sacrifice at your property, office, etc., it could indicate evil or demonic efforts that people are making to bring you down.

It also shows the extent to which people oppose you and the price they are prepared to pay in order to hinder you concerning certain matters.

It could equally mean that the forces of darkness have been engaged regarding a certain issue before you.

EXODUS 34:15; HEBREWS 12:24

Prayer Point

Use the Name and the Blood of Jesus to cancel and nullify any sacrifice that may be speaking against you, or speaking in your foundation, in Jesus' Name.

SAD

According to the Scriptures:

> **"Wherefore the king said unto me, Why is thy countenance sad, seeing thou art not sick? this is nothing else but sorrow of heart. Then I was very sore afraid"** (Nehemiah 2:2).

So when someone is sad in a dream, it is not good. It could mean that you are burdened by contemplating over matters of grave concern to you.

Prayer Point

NEHEMIAH 2:2

> **Bind and reject any spirit of sorrow and mourning on assignment against you and your family,** in Jesus' Name.

Prayer Point

EXODUS 12:29–30

> **Decree and declare that all those that want you to mourn or sorrow will never live to execute their plans, and command those spirits back to their senders,** in Jesus' Name.

SAILING

This is generally a good dream.

If you are sailing alone on calm waters, it could mean that good results await you, but there are elements of selfishness about you.

If you are sailing with others on calm water, it could equally mean that good fortune awaits you, as in the case of the apostles:

> **"And finding a ship sailing over unto Phenicia, we went aboard, and set forth. Now when we had discovered Cyprus, we left it on the left hand, and sailed into Syria, and landed at Tyre: for there the ship was to unlade her burden"** (Acts 21:2–3).

SALT

Generally speaking, anointed salt can expel evil spirits.

Salt in the dream speaks of healing and protective power. It could also represent the healing of your soul from affliction and bitterness, as the Prophet Elisha healed the bitter water:

> **"And he went forth unto the spring of the waters, and cast the salt in there, and said, Thus saith the LORD, I have healed these waters; there shall not be from thence any more death or barren land"** (2 Kings 2:21).

Further reading: 2 Chronicles 13:4–5

2 KINGS 2:19–22

Pray that God will heal every bitter situation in your life and turn them into sweetness that will glorify His name, in Jesus' Name.

SALUTE

Generally speaking, if a senior salutes a junior in a dream (for example, a father and his son), it could mean the senior is in error. He or she may have taken an action against you and may be trying to cover it up, as in the Scriptures when the King of Israel, Saul, saluted Samuel after he had presented an unlawful sacrifice to the Lord. Saul received the wrath of God for his actions (1 Samuel 13:9–13).

However, if you dream you are being saluted by military personnel, it could mean you will accomplish what you have set out to do and adversaries will not hinder you.

Conversely, if a policeman salutes you in a dream, it could mean that those fighting against you have given up.

SAND

To see a heap of sand in a dream means there is a need to work harder to achieve what is before you. Attaining things that should be yours may not be a smooth process.

The need to pray using the Word of God,

"for they shall suck of the abundance of the seas, and of treasures hid in the sand" (Deuteronomy 33:19), is paramount.

SATAN

This is the manifestation of a strong man or woman meant to oppose you and derail what God has ordained for you. In the Bible, Satan stood to resist Joshua (Zechariah 3:1), for Satan is the accuser, accusing us before our God day and night (Revelation 12:10).

ZECHARIAH 3:1

Prayer Point

> **Use the Name and the Blood of Jesus to resist, bind, and paralyse any strongman or strongwoman that is after you and possessed with the spirit of Satan; command the Angels of God to execute God's judgment upon them,** in Jesus' Name.

SATELLITE DISH

Generally speaking, this could symbolise a monitoring gadget fashioned against you.

Prayer: See prayers on LOOKING GLASS (MIRROR).

SCAFFOLD

If you are climbing a scaffold in the dream, it speaks of your desperate attempts to be heard.

SCHOOL

See **COLLEGE**

SCORPION

As the Word of God says,

> **"Behold, I give unto you power to tread on serpents and scorpions, and over all the power of the enemy: and nothing shall by any means hurt you"** (Luke 10:19),

so this is a negative dream.

Dreaming of scorpions indicates that your adversaries and enemies are not your equals but are very dangerous. They are deadly and effective at wreaking havoc. Do not underestimate them but deal with them decisively.

Further reading: 1 Kings 12:11

LUKE 10:19

Use the Name of Jesus to command the Angels of God to locate and frustrate any deadly enemy on assignment against you and your family; decree and declare that they will never live to execute their plans, in Jesus' Name.

SCRIPTURE (SEE BIBLE)

As the Bible says:

"And that from a child thou hast known the holy scriptures, which are able to make thee wise unto salvation through faith which is in Christ Jesus. All scripture is given by inspiration of God, and is profitable for doctrine, for reproof, for correction, for instruction in righteousness"
(2 Timothy 3:15–16).

When a Scripture is revealed to you in the dream, it could mean God is speaking to you about something you fear or doubt.

It also indicates the depth of your relationship in your spiritual walk with God.

SEA

See **OCEAN**

SEARCHING

According to the Scriptures, King Herod said,

> **"Go and search diligently for the young child; and when ye have found him, bring me word again"** (Matthew 2:8),

because he was troubled and distressed and thought Jesus would take his kingdom. When you are thoroughly searching for something in the dream and you cannot find it, it could mean that you are unnecessarily panicking over an issue you cannot easily share with anybody.

Further reading: Luke 15:8

SEAT

See **CHAIR**

SEDUCTION

As the Word of God says:

> **"Jezebel, which calleth herself a prophetess, to teach and to seduce my servants to commit fornication"** (Revelation 2:20).

Therefore, this is a negative dream.

If in the dream, you find that your junior is trying to seduce you, it could mean that you are being cautioned or warned to check your body language or relationship towards that person.

On the other hand, if you are the junior and you dream your senior seducing you, you must be cautioned about your conversations with them. You may be having filthy conversations.

REVELATION 2:20

Prayer Point

Use the Name and Blood of Jesus to bind and paralyse any spirit of Jezebel that may be in operation in your life or against you and your family, in Jesus' Name.

2 CORINTHIANS 6:14—15

Prayer Point

Use the Blood of Jesus to permanently separate yourself from any person that may be possessed with the spirit of Jezebel, in Jesus' Name.

SEED

According to the Bible:

"And God said, Behold, I have given you every herb bearing seed, which is upon the face of all the earth, and every tree, in the which is the fruit of a tree yielding seed; to you it shall be for meat" (Genesis 1:29).

To dream of seed is not only powerful but also revealing. It shows that your future or destiny is not only assured, but that the Hand of God is upon you, your efforts, and whatever you desire.

Further reading: Genesis 8:22

SELLING

See **MARKET**

SENATOR (LAWGIVER, LAWMAKER)

To dream you are a senator or are with senators speaks of positioning. In other words, you are going to be favoured in your chosen career. According to the Scriptures:

"And he provided the first part for himself, because there, in a portion of the lawgiver, was he seated; and he came with the heads

of the people, he executed the justice of the LORD, and his judgments with Israel" (Deuteronomy 33:21).

Further reading: Genesis 49:10

Prayer Point

DEUTERONOMY 33:21

Thank God for granting you the favour of God and man, and for placing you in a position of power, authority, influence, etc., to glorify His Name, in Jesus' Name.

SEPARATION

As the Scriptures say, it is sin and iniquities that separate us from God and hides His face from us (Isaiah 59:2). Therefore, being separated from your spouse, children, or beloved ones in a dream is not good. It could mean that there is on-going stress in your relationship that, if not checked, will lead to a disastrous end that will not be helpful at all.

Further reading: Proverbs 17:9

Prayer Point

ISAIAH 59:2

Ask God for mercy and to forgive you of every sin and iniquity that is causing you to be separated from what God has ordained for you, in Jesus' Name.

SERVANT

See **MAID**

SEX

This is generally an issue for both teenagers and adults. When you dream of sex, as a man or woman, with an unknown partner, it has many implications. It could indicate that you are very vulnerable in the realm of the spirit and that your flesh is susceptible to assault.

It could equally indicate the need to pray more and fight and bind the strong man or woman in your life, as the Word of God says:

> **"first bind the strong man? And then he will spoil his house"** (Matthew 12:29).

MATTHEW 12:29

Prayer Point

Use the Name and the Blood of Jesus to bind and paralyse any strongman or strongwoman in your life and in the lives of your family members; they will never live execute their evil plans, in Jesus' Name.

ISAIAH 8:10

Decree and declare that the activities and manipulations of strongmen and strongwomen over your life will never manifest, in Jesus' Name.

SHACKLES

See **CHAIN**

SHADOW

According to the Scriptures:

> "Before I go whence I shall not return, even to the land of darkness and the shadow of death; A land of darkness, as darkness itself; and of the shadow of death, without any order, and where the light is as darkness" (Job 10:21–22).

This is generally not a good dream.

When you see your shadow in the dream, you are being warned that things you have embarked on may bring calamity to you if you do not desist.

But when you see a shadow of a friend, relative, acquaintance, or someone else, you have to pray against the spirit of death.

Further reading: Psalm 23:4

Use the Name and the Blood of Jesus to bind and paralyse the spirit of death operating in your life and in the lives of your beloved ones, and command that spirit to return back to its sender, in Jesus' Name.

SHAME

See **ASHAMED**

SHAVING

See **HAIR**

SHEPHERD

As Jesus said,

> **"I am the good shepherd"** (John 10:14),

and

> **"the sheep hear his voice: and he calleth his own sheep by name, and leadeth them out"** (John 10:3).

This is a positive dream.

If you see yourself as a shepherd in the dream, it shows that you will be a great role model who will influence a lot of people. You will be a man or woman of power and authority.

SHIP

This is generally a good dream. It speaks of expansion and the growth of your territory or business ventures. Whatever you do will be very successful and will be connected with many nations, just as the Apostle Paul sailed abroad on a ship and grew his ministry as a result (Acts 21:2).

SHIPWRECK

As the Apostle Paul said:

> **"Thrice was I beaten with rods, once was I stoned, thrice I suffered shipwreck, a night and a day I have been in the deep"**
> (2 Corinthians 11:25).

Therefore, this is a negative dream.

It could mean that there will be a serious attack on your business, and steps must be taken immediately to prevent it.
Further reading: 1 Timothy 1:19

Prayer Point

2 CORINTHIANS 11:25

Use the Name and the Blood of Jesus to come against any attack of the enemy against your business, finances, and job; decree and declare that calamity will forever return back to all those projecting it against you and your beloved ones, in Jesus' Name.

SHOES

The meaning of this dream depends on the type of shoes.

New shoes signify a fresh position. If you are looking for or desiring something better than your current circumstances, this dream signifies a positive change, more so if the shoes are green, white, or brightly coloured.

Black, old, or tattered shoes symbolise frustration and exposure. You may experience setbacks.

If you choose a shoe that is not your size in the dream, it has a negative meaning. If the shoe is too small, it signifies that you are in a position that you should have moved on from. This could indicate that you are not ambitious. If the shoe is too big, you are over-ambitious and your efforts or desires are not realisable. You do not have the means to realise your goals.

Further reading: Exodus 3:5; Amos 2:6; Song of Solomon 7:1

DEUTERONOMY 25:9; JOB 20:27

Prayer Point

Command any projection of frustration and exposure to return to its sender; decree and declare that all those projecting frustration and exposure against you will never live to execute their plans, in Jesus' Name.

SHOOTING

Being shot in a dream is obviously a bad omen. There are two dimensions to this dream. Firstly, it could mean that some people have used words to assassinate your character and this may affect your position or character. As the psalmist said:

> **"Who whet their tongue like a sword, and bend their bows to shoot their arrows, even bitter words"** (Psalm 64:3).

Secondly, it could equally mean that your enemies have been using your name for enchantment and divination involving demonic or satanic arrows. The need for serious prayer is very important.

Mr. Alex came to me complaining that he was being shot at in a dream. Three months later, he narrowly missed a strange bullet that penetrated his bedroom. I believe that his fasting and prayer delivered him from this projectile that came from nowhere.

PSALM 64:3—4, 7; PSALM 37:14—15

Prayer Point

> **Decree and declare that anyone using your name for enchantment and divination in order to release satanic arrows against you will never live to execute their plans, and that their enchantment and divinations have failed and their arrows have returned back to their senders,** in Jesus' Name.

SHOWER

Generally speaking, to dream of showers is to dream of blessings. According to the Scriptures:

> **"and I will cause the shower to come down in his season; there shall be showers of blessing"** (Ezekiel 34:26).

To be under a shower could mean that you will have a favourable answer to a long-awaited desire, especially in your relationship.

It could equally mean that your efforts will be worthwhile.

Prayer Point

EZEKIEL 34:26

Thank God for the showers of blessing and favour that has been released upon your life, and decree that it shall ever manifest physically, in Jesus' Name.

SHRINE

As in the Bible:

> **"And they brought forth the images out of the house of Baal, and burned them. And they brake down the image of Baal, and brake down the house of Baal, and made it a draught house unto this day"**
> (2 Kings 10:26–27).

This speaks of the manifestation of household gods. If you find yourself at a shrine in the dream, it is a clear indication that your name, picture, clothing, belongings, or body parts (such as your hair or nails) have been taken to a shrine and the need to fast and pray is vital.

Further reading: Judges 17:5; Acts 19:24

Prayer Point

JUDGES 17:5; 2 KINGS 10:26–27

Command the Holy Ghost Fire of God to locate and destroy any shrine that may have the names, images, clothing, etc., of you and your family members for evil. Also, decree and declare that all those that have taken your personal effects to any shrine for evil will never live to execute their plans, but let the Angels of God locate them for judgment, in Jesus' Name.

SICKNESS

See **ILLNESS**

SIGHING

According to the Scriptures:

"Sigh therefore, thou son of man, with the breaking of thy loins; and with bitterness sigh before their eyes" (Ezekiel 21:6–7).

Therefore, this is an indication of bitterness of spirit. To sigh in a dream state could indicate there is an issue you have great misgivings about, although you are pretending everything is fine. Deep down, you are not comfortable, but there is nothing you can do because of your current situation.

SILVER

According to the Scriptures:

> **"Abram was very rich in cattle, in silver, and in gold"** (Genesis 13:2).

Therefore, this is a positive dream.

To see silver in the dream indicates general acceptance. Many people – both friends and foes – cannot help but appreciate what you are currently doing.

It could equally indicate that what you are currently doing will be blessed.

Additionally, it could symbolise business and financial success.

SINGING

In the Scriptures, as a result of victory over enemies, the Philistines, the women of Israel came out of the cities singing and dancing (1 Samuel 18:6). Therefore, if you dream you are singing, it is a sign of triumph over a current issue. No matter the situation you are in, it could mean victory has come.

2 CHRONICLES 20:22–23; JOSHUA 6:20

Thank God for granting you victory over your enemies and for causing you to triumph over every challenging situation that you may be facing. Decree that the victory that God has granted you is permanent and must come into manifestation, in Jesus' Name.

SINGLE

From my own perspective, when you are married and dream that you are single, it is warning to be careful of being distracted by casual appreciation of your physical appearance. You must not give flesh room to come into your marriage, for as Apostle Paul says in the Scriptures:

> **"But if they cannot control themselves, they should marry, for it is better to marry than to burn with passion"** (1 Corinthians 7:9, *NIV*).

Additionally, beware of divorce, for as Apostle Paul says:

> **"And unto the married I command, yet not I, but the Lord, Let not the wife depart from her husband: But and if she depart, let her**

remain unmarried, or be reconciled to her husband: and let not the husband put away his wife... Art thou bound unto a wife? seek not to be loosed. Art thou loosed from a wife? seek not a wife"

(1 Corinthians 7:10–11, 27).

MARK 10:9; 1 CORINTHIANS 7:10—11, 27

Prayer Point

Use the Name and the Blood of Jesus to nullify and command every projection of separation and divorce to return back to their senders; decree that those who want your marriage to break down will never live to execute their plans, in Jesus' Name.

SLAPPING (SMITE)

According to the Scriptures,

"Zedekiah the son of Chenaanah went near, and smote Micaiah on the cheek"
(1 Kings 22:24),

This is a negative dream.

When you are slapped in a dream, it indicates your enemies

are determined to attack you, and there is need for serious fasting and prayer.

However, if you are slapping someone in the dream, there is a need to check your temper and actions against subordinates or juniors in your home or workplace.

Further reading: John 19:3; Exodus 21:15

1 KINGS 22:24

Prayer Point

> **Command the Angels of God to rise up against all those that have arisen to attack you; decree and declare that any attack of the enemy against you shall forever fail, and those that will attempt to attack you will never live to execute their plans,** in Jesus' Name.

SLEEPING

To sleep in a dream is negative.

If you are asleep, you are being warned about your attitude to something that you should have acted on but chose to ignore.

If others are sleeping, it shows they are spiritually laid back or passive. Jesus told his disciples to pray lest they enter into temptation whilst he went yonder and prayed, but when he came back, they were sleeping (Luke 22:40–45).

SMOKE

In general, to see smoke in a dream could indicate that a negative aura is being released to hinder your wellbeing.

Prayer Point

EZEKIEL 8:11; NUMBERS 23:23

Use the Name and the Blood of Jesus to nullify any negative aura or atmosphere being projected against you and your family members, and command them to return back to their senders, in Jesus' Name.

If you dream of smoking, it is a warning that you are socialising with people who are spiritually opposed to you – your spirit is being polluted.

Prayer Point

2 CORINTHIANS 6:17

Use the Blood of Jesus to cancel, nullify, and separate yourself from anything in your life that is causing any form of spiritual pollution, in Jesus' Name.

SNAIL

The Bible categorises this animal as unclean (Leviticus 11:29–30). Therefore, this dream is negative.

To see a snail indicates that extreme frustration is about to come your way. There is a need to pray about it.

Further reading: Psalm 58:8

PSALM 58:8; MATTHEW 18:18

Bind and paralyse any spirit or projection of frustration, regression, and 'go-slow' that has been released against you, and command them to return back to their senders, in Jesus' Name.

SNAKE

See **ADDER**

SNEEZING

This is a positive dream.

If you are sick in real life and find yourself sneezing in a dream, it is confirmation of your complete healing or deliverance. When Elisha healed the dead child of the Shunammite woman, she sneezed seven times and that confirmed her revival (2 Kings 4:35).

If you are contemplating a specific issue, sneezing in a dream could mean a complete breakthrough.

SNOW

From my own perspective, snow in the dream could indicate that one may not speedily get what he/she desires. It is a moment in which you will be in a helpless circumstance as the moment unfolds.

MATTHEW 18:18

Prayer Point

Use the Name and the Blood of Jesus to bind and paralyse any frustrating spirit that may be in operation in your life; command the spirit to return back to its sender, in Jesus' Name.

SOLDIER

This is a good dream.

If you are a civilian in real life and you dream of being well dressed in military uniform, it could mean you are being called to a new duty.

Nevertheless, if you are a Christian, it could mean that you should become a worker in the House of God, as the Bible says:

> "therefore endure hardness, as a good soldier of Jesus Christ. No man that warreth entangleth himself with the affairs of this life; that he may please him who hath chosen him to be a soldier" (2 Timothy 2:3–4).

SOWING

According to the Word of God:

"And he that reapeth receiveth wages, and gathereth fruit unto life eternal: that both he that soweth and he that reapeth may rejoice together" (John 4:36).

This is a positive dream.

When you are sowing seeds in an open field, it generally signifies that your efforts in planting a new branch in a fresh location will be fruitful and prosperous.

SPIDER

According to the Scriptures:

"Whose hope shall be cut off, and whose trust shall be a spider's web" (Job 8:14).

This is a negative dream.

It could mean that there is a systematic effort to hinder whatever you are doing, especially from those you trust who are close to you.

JOB 8:14

Prayer Point

Use the Name and the Blood of Jesus to come against any conspiracy of the enemy (household enemies, unfriendly friends, etc.) to hinder and frustrate you, in Jesus' Name.

SPIRITS

See **GHOSTS**

SPITTING

This dream could go either way.

If you spit something out in a dream, it has serious spiritual implications. It could mean that self-deliverance has taken place. If you have been praying, you have been liberated from the source of your problem.

ISAIAH 49:25

Prayer Point

Thank God for delivering you from the hold and bondage of the enemy, and decree that that deliverance is permanent and shall come into manifestation, in Jesus' Name.

According to the Scriptures, when Jesus was arrested, He was spat on (Luke 18:32). Therefore, if someone spits at you, it signifies hatred. You cannot use love to win such a person.

Conversely, if you are spitting at someone, it portrays the depth of your hatred towards them. This must be checked.

Prayer Point

LUKE 18:32

> **Pray that all those who hate you and are plotting for your destruction will never live to execute their plans. Command the Angels of God to forever frustrate their plans and to execute God's judgment upon them,** in Jesus' Name.

SPLENDOUR

According to the Word of God:

> **"And your fame spread among the nations on account of your beauty, because the splendor I had given you made your beauty perfect, declares the Sovereign LORD"**
> (Ezekiel 16:14, *NIV*).

If you dream of yourself in splendour, it is a good omen. It signifies the time of your favour and manifestation has come.

EZEKIEL 16:14, PSALM 102:13

Thank God because the time of your favour has arrived, in Jesus' Name.

STAIRS

Stairs in the dream indicate the level or effort that will be taken towards the attainment of goals.

If you are climbing stairs effortlessly, it shows you will not labour in vain. It also indicates that provisions have been made to move you to the next level.

If you are climbing a staircase with difficulty, it could mean that much effort must be made before you achieve success. The exertion may not equal the outcome, and thus you are more likely to abandon what you are doing.

ISAIAH 65:23

Decree and declare that you will not labour in vain, and use the Name and the Blood of Jesus to bind and paralyse any power assigned to frustrate your efforts and to cause you to labour in vain; let them forever return to their senders, in Jesus' Name.

STARS

According to the Scriptures, the wise men knew about Jesus's birth and His position as the King of the Jews through his star (Matthew 2:1).

If you are looking at a bright star in a dream, it symbolises your future and could mean that whatever you embark on will be successful.

However, if the star is about to be covered, or is covered, you are being warned that the enemy wants to frustrate your efforts in achieving greatness.

Further reading: 1 Corinthians 15:41

MATTHEW 2:7–8; ISAIAH 25:7

Prayer Point

> **Decree and declare that all those that are fighting your star will never live to execute their plans; the Angels of God will locate them for judgment. Also, cancel and nullify any veil or cloud that has been placed over your star to cover your greatness,** in Jesus' Name.

STEALING

The Word of God states:

"Thou shalt not steal" (Exodus 20:15).

This is one of the commandments given to Moses. Apostle

Paul said in the Scriptures:

> **"Let him that stole steal no more: but rather let him labour, working with his hands the thing which is good, that he may have to give to him that needeth"** (Ephesians 4:28).

Therefore, this is a negative dream.

If you are caught stealing in the dream, you are being warned of something you have done that you thought was secret but is about to be exposed.

If you see someone stealing, it shows they are dishonest and insincere.

STEEL

Generally speaking, to dream of steel speaks of strength and resolution — it symbolises the dreamer's personality and sense of conviction over an issue.

STICK

See **CANE**

STONE

Stones are spiritual weapons. They are instruments of judgment that are used to kill giants in the realm of the spirit. David killed the giant, Goliath, with a stone (1 Samuel 17:49).

If someone is throwing stones at you in a dream, it indicates that they are trying to destroy your gigantic ideas or projects.

If you are throwing stones, it could mean that you want to bring judgment to the giants before you.

PROVERBS 26:17

Prayer Point

> **Use the Name of Jesus to command the Angel of God to return any stone of affliction, shame, death, etc., that has been rolled or thrown against you back to its sender,** in Jesus' Name.

1 SAMUEL 17:49

Prayer Point

> **Command the Angels of God to release stones of judgment upon every giant, strongman or strongwoman that is fighting and opposing you and your family,** in Jesus' Name.

STORE

From my own perspective, to see a full store is a positive dream. This indicates that you are applying wisdom in whatsoever you are doing and you will not regret your decisions and actions.

STORM

According to the Word of God:

"a tempest of hail and a destroying storm, as a flood of mighty waters overflowing, shall cast down to the earth with the hand"
(Isaiah 28:2).

This is a bad dream, and it signifies an unexpected attack concerning your office, relationships, or actions. It could be destructive, although it may last for a short while.

ISAIAH 28:2

Prayer Point

Use the Name and the Blood of Jesus to bind any turbulent spirit or any stormy situation that the enemy is trying to project into your life; command those projections back to their senders, in Jesus' Name.

SUICIDE

From my own perspective, if you or someone you know commits suicide in the dream, it could mean that evil spirits want to take hold of the person as a result of current difficulties or circumstances.

Prayer Point

> Bind and paralyse any evil spirit that is on assignment to possess you and cover you in darkness; command them to return back to their senders, in Jesus' Name.

EXODUS 12:12—13

Prayer Point

> Use the Blood of Jesus to permanently draw a bloodline between any evil and ungodly spirit and yourself, in Jesus' Name.

SUN

This dream could be either positive or negative.

The rising of the sun in the dream speaks of greatness in your life's endeavour. You will be a source of blessing to those who come across you. According to the Scriptures:

> **"And for the precious fruits brought forth by the sun"** (Deuteronomy 33:14).

Nevertheless, if the sun is setting, it is a warning about a reversal of your circumstances.
   Further reading: Isaiah 60:20

PSALM 121:6

Decree and declare that any person using the powers of the sun to fight you, your family, and your blessings will never live to execute their plans; any projection made to the sun against you and your family will forever **backfire,** in Jesus' Name.

ISAIAH 60:20

Use the Name of Jesus to command the Angels of God to locate and frustrate all those that want to cause your sun to go down; their own suns shall go down on your **behalf,** in Jesus' Name.

SWEARING

This is a negative dream.

If you dream that someone you know is swearing at you, it shows that the state of his or her heart towards you is not good. In reality, he or she is false with regard to your relationship.

PROVERBS 26:26; MATTHEW 15:13

Prayer Point

Ask God to reveal and expel any unfriendly friend, or those around you not planted by God, from your life, in Jesus' Name.

On the other hand, if you are the one swearing, it shows the degree of your fear and frustration over an issue, as in the Scriptures when Peter was scared of being arrested, he swore not knowing Jesus (see Mark 14:71).

MARK 14:71; 2 TIMOTHY 1:7

Prayer Point

Use the Name and the Blood of Jesus to bind and paralyse every spirit of fear and frustration in your life. Also, cancel and reject any frustrating or fearful situation the enemy has projected into your life, and return them back to their senders, in Jesus' Name.

T

TABLE

As the psalmist proclaimed:

"Thou preparest a table before me in the presence of mine enemies" (Psalm 23:5).

This dream has mixed interpretations depending on the colour, size, and height of the table. It generally signifies a promotion.

When you see a golden table in a dream, it could mean that blessings, promotions, etc., before you came about as a result of severe trials and temptations. No one can take them from you.

If you see a silver table, it signifies you are entering your rest in your place of blessing.

Prayer Point

PSALM 23:5

Thank God for your table of promotion, blessings, fruitfulness, healing, favour, miracles, etc., and claim it. Also, thank God because the time for your table of blessings to manifest has come and no enemy shall prevail against it, in Jesus' Name.

If the table is not strong, it could mean that a forthcoming promotion will not last.

If the table is broken or dirty it could mean that a promotion will not be a blessing to you and you will face difficulties.

Further reading: Psalm 69:22; 1 Kings 4:27; Luke 22:29–30

Prayer Point

MATTHEW 18:18; PSALM 69:22

Bind every power of darkness assigned to fight or hinder your table. Also, decree that that the Angels of God will bring the judgment of God upon any person or Judas who will be assigned to steal away your table of blessings, in Jesus' Name.

TAIL

The Bible says:

> **"And the LORD shall make thee the head, and not the tail; and thou shalt be above only, and thou shalt not be beneath"**
> (Deuteronomy 28:13).

Therefore, to see yourself at the tail end of any queue in a dream is negative. It could mean that you have a long journey before you concerning present issues.

DEUTERONOMY 28:13

Thank God because He has made you the head and not the tail in every situation of your life. Therefore, bind and paralyse every spirit of 'the tail' that has been assigned to fight you from succeeding, and command them back to their senders, in Jesus' Name.

TATTOO

The Bible warns about tattoos,

"Do not cut your bodies for the dead or put tattoo marks on yourselves. I am the LORD"
(Leviticus 19:28, *NIV*),

so this is a negative dream.

If you do not have tattoos and you dream of having them, it could symbolise caution about your desire to do as others do when it is not necessary.

Prayer: See prayers on MARK.

TEARS

This is a contrary dream. It could mean that God has intervened in the realm of the spirit and you will eventually overcome the issues that are giving you sleepless nights. The

Scriptures say:

> **"And God shall wipe away all tears from their eyes; and there shall be no more death, neither sorrow, nor crying, neither shall there be any more pain: for the former things are passed away"** (Revelation 21:4).

TEETH

As the psalmist proclaimed:

> **"Break their teeth, O God, in their mouth: break out the great teeth of the young lions, O LORD"** (Psalm 58:6).

This is generally not a good dream.

Dreaming of teeth could mean that negative words spoken to others have eaten deep into their emotions and affected them.

If you are brushing your teeth, it could mean you regret words you have spoken and are trying to make amends.

As a young person, if you dream your teeth are falling out, this could be a self-imposed curse – things you have said in the past have come to haunt you.

Further reading: Acts 7:54

TELESCOPE

Generally speaking, this is a negative dream. You are being warned of people monitoring you.

Prayer: See prayers on LOOKING GLASS (MIRROR).

TELEVISION

From my perspective, a television in a dream could mean you will have a sudden emergency, either positive or negative.

However, if you see yourself on television, it is a positive dream that could mean great acceptance by a wider audience.

TEMPTATION

As the Word of God says:

"lead us not into temptation, but deliver us from evil" (Matthew 6:13).

This is a dream of what is to come and speaks of matters burning in your heart. This could be something you have set your mind to do despite the consequences.

It could equally mean that the enemy is lurking, intending to lay a snare.

1 SAMUEL 18:21; PSALM 124:7

Decree that any enemy planning to ensnare you will never live to execute their plans: let them be caught in their own wicked snares and nets, in Jesus' Name.

TENANTS

According to the Scriptures:

> **"when the tenants saw him, they talked the matter over. 'This is the heir,' they said. 'Let's kill him, and the inheritance will be ours'"** (Luke 20:14, *NIV*).

If you are a landlord and you dream of being a tenant in your own house, it could it could be a warning of a reversal of fortune.

TEACHER

This is usually a good dream.

If you are not in the teaching profession but you dream of being a teacher, it could mean that circumstances will cause you to be in a position where your counsel, advice, and ideas will be of great help to those around you.

However, if you are in the teaching profession, this dream could mean much is expected from you and you are not doing your best in your current circumstances.

If you are of school age and dream of being a teacher, it could mean that you will have a promising future. Your teachers and classmates will come to recognise your resourcefulness. As the psalmist said:

"I have more understanding than all my teachers" (Psalm 119:99).

PSALM 119:99

Prayer Point

Decree and declare, using the Name of Jesus, that you and your children shall have more wisdom and understanding than all your teachers, in Jesus' Name.

TERMINAL ILLNESS

According to the Scriptures, Hezekiah was sick unto death. Having been informed he would die, he sought God's face through prayers, and God answered him by extending his lifespan (Isaiah 38:1–5). When you dream of a terminal illness, it is negative.

It is important to fast and pray and to seek spiritual counsel.

1 PETER 2:24; EXODUS 15:26

Bind and reject every terminal illness and return it back to its sender, in Jesus' Name.

TERROR

This dream could go either way.

If you see a terrifying figure in the dream, it clearly depicts an evil spirit who is after you. There is need to bind them, for the Word of God says:

"Thou shalt not be afraid for the terror by night" (Psalm 91:5).

However, if you are the source of terror in the dream, it could mean you are confronting a strong man or woman who is oppressing your beloved ones.

PSALM 91:5

Use the Name and the Blood of Jesus to bind and paralyse every terror of the night assigned against you, and command them to return back to their senders, in Jesus' Name.

TEST (DRIVING)

From my own perspective, if you are taking a driving test in the dream, it could mean that your present occupation will be tested. For according to the Scriptures:

> **"Wherein ye greatly rejoice, though now for a season, if need be, ye are in heaviness through manifold temptations: That the trial of your faith, being much more precious than of gold that perisheth, though it be tried with fire, might be found unto praise and honour and glory at the appearing of Jesus Christ"** (1 Peter 1:6–7).

However, if you are a licenced driver and you dream of taking a driving test, it could be a warning to drive cautiously so your licence will not be revoked or suspended as a result of serious carelessness on your part.

TEXT MESSAGE

Generally, any text message you receive in a dream should be taken seriously. It could either be a warning or a piece of advice.

THANKSGIVING

This is a positive dream. It means all-round victory, as the

Word of God said:

"And out of them shall proceed thanksgiving and the voice of them that make merry: and I will multiply them, and they shall not be few; I will also glorify them, and they shall not be small" (Jeremiah 30:19).

JEREMIAH 30:19

Thank God for multiplying you, glorifying you, and making you great, in Jesus' Name.

THIEF

According to the Word of God:

"The thief cometh not, but for to steal, and to kill, and to destroy: I am come that they might have life, and that they might have it more abundantly" (John 10:10).

This is a negative dream.

When you dream you are hiding from a thief in your house, it could mean there is a household member you do not like and you are not willing to associate with them.

JOHN 10:10

> **Command the Angels of God to locate and frustrate any man or woman wanting to steal, kill, or destroy your blessings and that of your family members; let God's judgment come upon them,** in Jesus' Name.

THIRST

If you keep dreaming of being thirsty, it could mean that you need to set aside more time or carry out greater research into a project or task.

For example, Christians need to desire more of the things of God, as Jesus answered the woman at the well:

> **"Whosoever drinketh of this water shall thirst again"** (John 4:13).

THREAT

This is a negative dream.

If you dream you are being threatened, it could be mean you must beware of the spirit of fear, just as when the Jews wanted to threaten Peter and John in order to inflict the spirit of fear in them so they would not preach in the name of Jesus (Acts 4:17).

However, if you are threatening someone, it could mean you are cautiously handling an issue that is promoting fear instead of love.

Prayer Point

ACTS 4:29; 2 TIMOTHY 1:7

> **Bind and reject the spirit of fear. Pray for God to give you the boldness and power to overcome every threat of the enemy,** in Jesus' Name.

THRONE

This is generally a dream of success, power, and authority. According to the Scriptures:

> **"Moreover the king made a great throne of ivory, and overlaid it with the best gold"**
> (1 Kings 10:18).

If you see yourself relaxed on a throne, it could mean you are firmly established.

If you are before a throne and you are troubled, it could mean that you need to repent of your acts and deeds.

Further reading: Proverbs 20:8

1 SAMUEL 2:8

Pray that God will set you among princes and cause you to inherit a throne of glory, in Jesus' Name.

TOAD

See **FROG**

TOBACCO

See **SMOKE, SMOKING**

TOILET

Generally speaking, this dream could go either way.

To be in your toilet in the dream is positive, it symbolises being in control of domestic pressures.

However, dreaming of being in someone else's toilet is negative. It could mean that problems concerning you are known to others close to you, but they are not willing to let you know.

TOMB

SEE **GRAVE**

TORTOISE

The Bible classifies this animal as unclean (Leviticus 11:29). Therefore, a dream of a tortoise is negative.

It could mean that your current problems or frustrations are the result of deceitful counsel from trusted friends.

Prayer Point

LEVITICUS 11:29

Use the Name and the Blood of Jesus to cancel and nullify every projection of uncleanliness, 'go-slow', and frustration made against you and your family, in Jesus' Name.

TOWEL (LOINCLOTH)

According to the Bible:

"Thus saith the LORD unto me, Go and get thee a linen girdle, and put it upon thy loins, and put it not in water. So I got a girdle according to the word of the LORD, and put it on my loins" (Jeremiah 13:1–2).

To wear a towel around you in your house could show a degree of relaxation over domestic challenges and issues before you.

But to dream of wearing a towel in a public place could symbolise that an enemy wants to expose you and see your nakedness.

TOWER

This is a positive dream. If you see yourself in a tower, it speaks of great height in both spiritual matters and your area of expertise.

It equally could mean you are spiritually watchful. As it says in the Scriptures:

> **"And there stood a watchman on the tower in Jezreel, and he spied the company of Jehu as he came"** (2 Kings 9:17).

Prayer Point

DEUTERONOMY 7:13; PSALM 115:14

Thank God for taking you to new heights in your business, in your studies, in your marriage, in your spiritual life, etc., and pray that He will give you the grace to aim for even greater heights, in Jesus' Name.

TRAFFIC

This is usually not a good dream as it symbolises hindrances on your way.

If you dream of being stuck in traffic, it could mean that your enemies have succeeded in stopping you.

On the other hand, if there is traffic and your vehicle is moving, it could mean that you are still succeeding despite the attempts of your enemies to stop you.

JOSHUA 1:5

Prayer Point

Pray for the removal of every hindrance or obstacle that is hindering your progress; thank God for promoting movement in any area of your life where you have come to a standstill, despite the attempts of the enemy to hinder you, in Jesus' Name.

TRAGEDY

In general, this is a negative dream. It shows your adversaries are imagining evil against you. But if you pray, you could cancel it, for the Bible says:

> **"There hath no temptation taken you but such as is common to man: but God is faithful, who will not suffer you to be tempted above that ye are able; but will**

with the temptation also make a way to escape, that ye may be able to bear it" (1 Corinthians 10:13).

1 CORINTHIANS 10:13; PROVERBS 21:18

Cancel every evil imagination of the wicked ones fashioned against you, your family, your marriage, your business, etc., using the Name and the Blood of Jesus Christ. Pray that their evil desires will ever backfire upon them and their own households, in Jesus' Name.

TRAIN (LOCOMOTION)

This is a dream of movement, with different levels of challenges and oppositions. However, if you are steadfast, you will overcome. Although it may take a long time, eventually the situation will be in your favour.

2 TIMOTHY 2:3—6; LUKE 2:52

Ask God for a steadfast spirit and to enable you to overcome challenges and setbacks that you may be facing in your particular situation; pray for God to grant you favour, in Jesus' Name.

TRAIN (BRIDAL)

If you are unmarried and you dream of wearing a bridal train, it is an indication of a wedding, although there might be hitches along the way.

TRAP (SNARE)

The psalmist prayed:

"Keep me from the snares which they have laid for me" (Psalm 141:9).

If you see a trap in the dream, it could mean that your enemies are planning something or you are under pressure to do something that is a trick to get to you and destroy your success.

Further reading: Exodus 34:12

Prayer Point

PSALM 141:9; PSALM 35:8

Pray that no snare laid by the enemy to destroy your joy, your success, your health, etc., shall ever entrap you; pray for all those laying evil snares to become victims of their own wicked devices, in Jesus' Name.

TREE

The Bible states,

> **"Even so every good tree bringeth forth good fruit; but a corrupt tree bringeth forth evil fruit. A good tree cannot bring forth evil fruit, neither can a corrupt tree bring forth good fruit. Every tree that bringeth not forth good fruit is hewn down, and cast into the fire"** (Matthew 7:17–19).

This dream could go either way.

If you see a tree that is green and bearing fruit, it shows that your current efforts will be prosperous. Your relationship or marriage will abound in love and good fortune, for the Word of God says:

> **"he shall be like a tree planted by the rivers of water, that bringeth forth his fruit in his season; his leaf also shall not wither; and whatsoever he doeth shall prosper"**
> (Psalm 1:3).

PSALM 1:3

Prayer Point

Thank God for causing your efforts to become prosperous and bear fruits in all aspects of your life e.g. in your marriage, in your business, in your studies, in Jesus' Name.

If you see a tree without fruits even though it is the time of fruitfulness, you need to pray against the powers of darkness that are fighting the manifestation of your blessings.

If the tree is dry, this signifies that there is a curse promoting aridness in your business, relationship, or marriage, and the need to cancel it is important.

Further reading: Jeremiah 1:11–12

JEREMIAH 1:11–12

Prayer Point

Pray that any fruitless tree that the enemy is using to promote poverty, failure, lack, want, barrenness, marital problems, etc., be consumed by the heavenly Fire of God. Also, cancel every curse that the enemy has made using evil trees, and return them back to their senders, in Jesus' Name.

TRIPLETS

From my personal ministration, to dream of triplets is very prophetic.

If a woman with children in real life dreams of triplets, it could mean fruitfulness and abundance of blessings. It could also mean that her children will never suffer lack.

GENESIS 1:28

> **If you are not seeking the fruit of the womb, thank God for His confirmation of blessing and fruitfulness for your life and that of your children,** in Jesus' Name.

On the other hand, if she is barren and dreams of triplets, what is being revealed is that someone has cursed her womb. The need to pray against the wickedness of this is vital.

HOSEA 9:14; EXODUS 23:26

> **If you are seeking the fruit of the womb, use the Name and the Blood of Jesus to nullify and reverse any curse, enchantment, or incantation that has ever been made to cause your womb to be barren; pray for God to open your womb,** in Jesus' Name.

TROPHY

This is generally a positive dream. According to the Scriptures:

> **"the LORD their God shall save them in that day as the flock of his people: for they shall be as the stones of a crown, lifted up as an ensign upon his land"** (Zechariah 9:16).

It indicates that your efforts in whatever you are doing will have surprising results.

Prayer Point

ZECHARIAH 9:16

Thank God for giving you the victory in all your circumstances, and for honouring your efforts, in Jesus' Name.

TROUSERS

See **CLOTHING**

TRUMPET

From my own perspective, to hear a trumpet in a dream could be a warning. For example, when the Prophet Isaiah was proclaiming against Ethiopia saying:

"All ye inhabitants of the world, and dwellers on the earth, see ye, when he lifteth up an ensign on the mountains; and when he bloweth a trumpet, hear ye" (Isaiah 18:3).

Conversely, trumpets can also announce your success and glories – good news that will go beyond your immediate environment.

TUNNEL

In general, if you dream of going through a tunnel, it could mean that you are being shown that success will not come easily. If you persist, eventually the time of an open door will come.

Further reading: 2 Kings 20:20

Prayer Point

2 KINGS 20:20; 1 CORINTHIANS 16:9

Pray that God should give you the strength and the grace to persist through times of trials and tribulations so that the enemy does not frustrate and discourage you at the point of reaching your open doors, in Jesus' Name.

TWINS

This shows the power of confirmation. You will eventually have that which you desire earnestly because 'two' is a number of confirmations.

Prayer Point

GENESIS 37:7, 9; GENESIS 41:32

> Use the Name and the Blood of Jesus to claim any good dream that God has revealed unto you twice, as that dream has been ordained to come to pass, in Jesus' Name.

Prayer Point

ISAIAH 60:2; GENESIS 41:32

> Use the Name and the Blood of Jesus to cancel any negative dream that has been revealed unto you twice, and paralyse the forces of darkness promoting those evil dreams, in Jesus' Name.

U

UMBILICAL CORD

As in the Scriptures:

> **"On the day you were born, no one cared about you. Your umbilical cord was not cut"** (Ezekiel 16:1–4, *NLT*).

This is an uncommon dream that means that issues before you are linked to your foundation – there is a need for you to separate yourself from anything that is not of God.

EZEKIEL 16:1—4

Prayer Point

Use the Name and the Blood of Jesus to separate yourself from anything not of God in your foundation, and command them to be destroyed by the Fire of God, in Jesus' Name.

UNDERGROUND

This is obviously a bad dream. It could mean that the forces contending with you are determined to hinder you, and if possible, frustrate you forever. There is a need for serious deliverance prayers. As the Scripture shows in 1 Samuel 28:13:

"I saw gods ascending out of the earth."

UNDERTAKER

This is a negative dream.

To see an undertaker in the dream signifies problems, issues, and challenges are still at their beginning stages. If care is not taken, it will be much more disastrous than you think.
   Further reading: Amos 6:9–10

UNDRESSING

See **NAKEDNESS**

UNIVERSITY

Generally, dreams involving university could have the following interpretations.

   If you dream you are in a university before getting admission into that university in real life, it could mean that if you study hard and do not get distracted, you will be admitted there.

   If you are in university in real life, dreaming about it means the need to take your studies more seriously is very important.

   If you are a graduate and see yourself back at university, it could mean that the enemy is fighting to keep you behind.

JEREMIAH 3:22; MATTHEW 18:18

> **Use the Name and the Blood of Jesus to bind and paralyse any power of regression on assignment against you; command those powers to return back to their senders,** in Jesus' Name.

URINE

This is a common dream.

Prosaically, it often means your urinary tract is under pressure and you need to wake up to ease yourself.

However, if you are an adult and you urinate in bed, assuming you were in the toilet, there is need to pray against shame being projected on you.

PSALM 109:29

> **Use the Name and the Blood of Jesus to come against any spirit or projection of shame that has been released against you, and command those spirits and projections to return back to their senders. Decree that all those who want you to be ashamed will forever be clothed with shame on your behalf,** in Jesus' Name.

V

VACATION

See **HOLIDAY**

VALLEY

This is a negative dream.

To dream of a valley is a warning that a decision you want to take may bring you down.

If you are in the valley, it could mean that you need God's intervention in the problem you are facing in order to be delivered. The need to go into fasting and prayer is important. As the psalmist said:

> **"Yea, though I walk through the valley of the shadow of death, I will fear no evil: for thou art with me; thy rod and thy staff they comfort me"** (Psalm 23:4).

Before I became born again, as a bank manager, I dreamt that I saw two of my valued customers in a valley. I shared the dream with them, and we joked over it. Less than six months later, they did two business transactions with Chinese men, and the goods they received were less than the value they expected. This marked the beginning of problems that brought huge losses to them.

They were not able to service the loan the bank had given to them, and eventually, their properties held by the bank as collateral had to be sold. In 2006, I saw one of them in London. He told me that he wanted to commit suicide and was begging for bread because of the failure and shame. He had left Nigeria to do menial jobs in London.

PSALM 23:4

Prayer Point

> **Pray that all those that are projecting valley-like situations into your life and the lives of your family members will never live to execute their plans; those that want you to dwell in a valley will remain in such valleys in your stead,** in Jesus' Name.

PSALM 91:11–12; PSALM 30:1

Prayer Point

> **Use the Name of Jesus to command the Angels of God to uplift you and your family from any valley of sickness, poverty, shame, stagnation, depression, etc., in which the enemy may have placed you,** in Jesus' Name.

VEHICLE

See **CAR**

VEIL

Dreaming of a veil can have different, significant meanings depending on its colour.

- A white veil signifies marriage.
- A black veil signifies death.
- A red veil signifies condemnation.
- A grey veil signifies sacrifice.

In general, veils talk of coverage by a stronger enemy, as in the Scriptures:

> **"And he will swallow up on this mountain the covering that is cast over all peoples, the veil that is spread over all nations"**
> (Isaiah 25:7, *ESV*).

Further reading: Exodus 34:29, 33

Prayer Point

ISAIAH 25:2

Use the Name of Jesus to command the Fire of God to consume any evil veil, cloud, or covering that the enemy has used to cover your star or the glory of God in your life, in Jesus' Name.

Prayer Point

ISAIAH 60:2

Use the Name and the Blood of Jesus to command the Angels of God to execute God's judgment upon all those that are trying to cover your star and your glory, in Jesus' Name.

VICTORY

This dream could be either good or bad.

If you dream you are victorious, it could mean that you are rejoicing over something you thought was hopeless. As the psalmist said:

> **"but you give us victory over our enemies, you put our adversaries to shame"**
> (Psalm 44:7, *NIV*).

PSALM 44:7

Prayer Point

Thank God for making you victorious over your enemies and every negative situation in your life, in Jesus' Name.

However, when you see your enemies rejoicing, it could mean that they may be successful in their plan so the need to pray is important.

VILLAGE

This dream can have two meanings.

If you are living in a village in real life and you see yourself in the city, it shows you have a strong desire to leave.

However, if you live in a town or city in real life and you dream of yourself idle in a village, it could mean that your challenges or issues are related to powers and authorities in the village trying to frustrate you. Like the Scripture says in Leviticus 25:31:

> "the houses of the villages which have no wall round about them… they may be redeemed, and they shall go out in the jubilee."

PSALM 30:1; PSALM 109:29

Prayer Point

Decree that all those that want to wrongfully rejoice over you will ever be put to shame, in Jesus' Name.

EPHESIANS 6:12

Prayer Point

Use the Name and the Blood of Jesus to bind and paralyse any territorial power of familiar spirit from your village, home town, and/or place of birth that are fighting you; command the Angels of God to execute God's judgment upon all those that are consulting with those powers in order to fight you, in Jesus' Name.

VIOLENCE

In most cases, you are being warned to be careful that a sudden attack may come upon whatever you are doing but will not endure.

Prayer Point **PSALM 37:23**

> **Ask God to order you steps so that you will not find yourself in the wrong place at the wrong time,** in Jesus' Name.

If you dream you are the victim of violence, there is a need for you to pray not to be in the wrong place at the wrong time.

As in the time of Noah in Genesis 6:13:

> **"And God said unto Noah, The end of all flesh is come before me; for the earth is filled with violence through them; and, behold, I will destroy them with the earth."**

Prayer Point **PSALM 37:14—15**

> **Decree that any attack of the enemy against you and loved ones should return back to their senders, and command the Angels of God to execute God's judgment upon all those that will ever plot to attack you,** in Jesus' Name.

408

VISITING

There are several interpretations of dreams of visiting.

Genesis 18:1–5 says:

> **"And the LORD appeared unto him in the plains of Mamre: and he sat in the tent door in the heat of the day; And he lift up his eyes and looked, and, lo, three men stood by him: and when he saw them, he ran to meet them from the tent door, and bowed himself toward the ground, And said, My Lord, if now I have found favour in thy sight, pass not away, I pray thee, from thy servant: Let a little water, I pray you, be fetched, and wash your feet, and rest yourselves under the tree: And I will fetch a morsel of bread, and comfort ye your hearts; after that ye shall pass on: for therefore are ye come to your servant. And they said, So do, as thou hast said."**

Therefore, if you are entertaining visitors you do not know with joy, it could mean that you may have a spiritual or prophetic encounter.

If you dream of close acquaintances visiting you, it could mean that you have to be wary in your dealings with such people.

If you have dead relatives visiting you, especially if you are eating with them, there is nothing good about this dream. The need to cancel the spirit of death is paramount, as Luke 24:5 says:

> **"And as they were afraid, and bowed down their faces to the earth, they said unto them, Why seek ye the living among the dead?"**

Some months after my father's death, one of my father's friends told my mother about a dream he had where he was with my father and they were being served as royalty. In the dream, my late father invited him to eat, whom he refused and said he would rather drink, and he was served drinks in a beautiful place. Due to his age, I felt I was not in a position to tell him it was a bad dream because he saw it otherwise. Six months later, he died. To dream of eating with a dead relative is negative; it speaks of a covenant with the realm of the dead.

LUKE 24:5; HOSEA 13:14

Prayer Point

Use the Name and the Blood of Jesus to cancel and nullify every spirit of death assigned against you and command them to return back to their senders, in Jesus' Name.

VOICES

Generally, if you see people that you know talking in the dream but you cannot hear what they are saying, it could mean that some of your close friends are gossiping about you.

Like the Scripture says in 1 Corinthians 14:10:

> **"There are, it may be, so many kinds of voices in the world, and none of them is without signification."**

If you hear a voice in the dream and the sound thereof is fearful, it could mean that there are people calling your name for evil enchantments.

Further reading: Judges 21:2

JUDGES 21:2; NUMBERS 23:23

Prayer Point

Use the Name and the Blood of Jesus to cancel and nullify any evil voice speaking against you and your family; decree and declare that any man or woman enchanting against you, their enchantments will forever backfire by fire, in Jesus' Name.

VOMITING

If you vomit in the dream but you do not feel sick when you wake up, it could mean great deliverance from spiritual contamination. As the Scripture says:

"The morsel which thou hast eaten shalt thou vomit up, and lose thy sweet words" (Proverbs 23:8).

Further reading: Proverbs 26:11

PROVERBS 23:8

Prayer Point

Thank God for giving you deliverance over any spiritual contamination, in Jesus' Name.

VOW

Usually, if you see yourself making a vow in the dream, it is serious – you need to keep that vow no matter how difficult it is. As the Word of God says: **"When thou vowest a vow unto God, defer not to pay it; for he hath no pleasure in fools: pay that which thou hast vowed. Better is it that thou shouldest not vow, than that thou shouldest vow and not pay"** (Ecclesiastes 5:4–5).

But if someone is making an evil vow against you, it could mean that a battle line has been drawn.

ISAIAH 28:15, 18

Decree and declare that all those that have gone into any evil vow, oath, or covenant to fight you and your family members will never live to accomplish their plans; let the Angels of God frustrate them and execute God's judgment upon them, in Jesus' Name.

VULTURE

Scripture classifies vultures as an abomination among the fowls (Leviticus 11:13–14). Therefore, a dream of a vulture is a negative one. From my counselling experience, such dreams show that enemies are projecting ugliness against you.

LEVITICUS 11:13—14

Use the Name and Blood of Jesus to cancel and nullify any projection of disfavour made against you, in Jesus' Name.

W

WALL

Walls talk of enclosure and limitation.

When you see yourself within walls and you are not making efforts to find your way out, it shows you have been limited spiritually.

Likewise, you may experience a long and frustrating period in your endeavours. There is a need to embark on fasting and prayers and seek spiritual help, like in the case of the Israelites who destroyed the Wall of Jericho – only through God's intervention, the walls collapsed (Joshua 6:1–20).

JOSHUA 6:20

Prayer Point

Use the Name of Jesus to command the Fire of the Holy Ghost to locate and destroy any wall of limitation that the enemy has placed in your life to keep you from achieving what God has ordained for you, in Jesus' Name.

WAR

According to Exodus 1:10:

> **"it come to pass, that, when there falleth out any war, they join also unto our enemies, and fight against us, and so get them up out of the land."**

War speaks of imminent danger that may cost lives or relationships and have drastic impacts and endings.

Equally, this dream could be a wakeup call to put your house in order, ready for inevitabilities that will confront you.

Prayer Point

EXODUS 1:10, ISAIAH 49:25

Use the Name and the Blood of Jesus to command the Angels of God to declare war on and contend with all those contending with you and your family members; all those that have risen up against you will never live to execute their plans, in Jesus' Name.

WAREHOUSE

See **STORE**

WASHING

See **LAUNDRY**

WATCH

According to the Scriptures:

"Behold, I will watch over them for evil, and not for good" (Jeremiah 44:27).

This dream can go either way.

If you dream you are keeping a watchful eye on people you know, it could mean that there is a decision or action you want to take but you are being careful.

Conversely, if you are watching strangers, it is an expository dream meaning there are those in your place of work or elsewhere that you are to keep a distance and avoid opening your heart to.

If others are watching you from afar, it could mean that there are people who want to undo you but don't know how to go about it.

WATER

See **DRINKING, RIVER, OCEAN**

WAVE

This is not usually a good dream.

When you are waving at people from the same household, it indicates decisions or actions you have taken or are about to take may be unpleasant in the short run, but there is nothing you can do about it.

If a person who is sick in reality is waving at you in the dream and you respond, the need to pray using,

> **"I shall not die, but live, and declare the works of the LORD"** (Psalm 118:17), is important.

PSALM 118:17; PROVERBS 21:18

Cancel and nullify any projection of death and of sickness that has been set over you and your family members; command them to return back to their senders, in Jesus' Name.

WEAPON

A weapon of any kind is generally not a good sign in a dream.

This is why the Scripture says:

"No weapon that is formed against you will prosper" (Isaiah 54:17, *NASB*).

However, it depends on who is carrying the weapon.

This indicates that there is a determined effort to cut you down prematurely:

"every man with his destroying weapon in his hand" (Ezekiel 9:1).

On the other hand, if you are the one carrying a weapon, it could mean that you are ready to confront a matter or issue that has been bothering you.

ISAIAH 54:17, EZEKIEL 9:1

Prayer Point

Decree and declare that any weapon of sickness, death, failure, poverty, etc., that has been fashioned against you and your loved ones shall not prosper; command them to ever return back to their senders, in Jesus' Name.

WEATHER

Generally speaking, if you experience different climate changes in the same dream, you must be careful of your thoughts on an inconclusive issue. It indicates that you should not act based on the information before you alone and that there is a need to seek spiritual guidance.

PROVERBS 3:5—6

Prayer Point

Pray that in any decision you're going to take, let God order your steps and let the Angels of God guide your path, in Jesus' Name.

WEDDING CLOTHES

Generally, this is a good dream.

If you are engaged in real life, and you dream of wedding

clothes, it could mean that despite the challenges and hiccups you and your partner may face, you will have a good wedding.

However, if you are not engaged but keep dreaming of these, it indicates there is a strong opposition towards your wedding goals or plans (Matthew 22:11–13).

WEDDING RING

From my own perspective, if you are married in real life but you dream you cannot find your wedding ring, it could mean that there may be faithfulness issues or doubts creeping into your marriage, and there is a need to pray about it.

If you are not married but dream you are wearing a wedding ring, it is likely to be an evil covenant with a spirit husband or wife.

Prayer Point

2 CORINTHIANS 6:14–15

Use the Name and the Blood of Jesus to bind and paralyse any spirit wife or spirit husband operating in your life; use the Blood of Jesus to separate yourself from any covenant with such spirits that are operating in your life, in Jesus' Name.

And, if you are unmarried and cannot find your wedding ring, it could mean strong forces are against any marriage plans you have – the marriage may experience attack.

EPHESIANS 6:12

Use the Name and the Blood of Jesus to bind and paralyse any power, authority, or throne of darkness that is fighting your marriage or marital plans; decree and declare that your marriage will never know frustration, in Jesus' Name.

WEED

According to the Scriptures,

> **"The owner's servants came to him and said, 'Sir, didn't you sow good seed in your field? Where then did the weeds come from?'"** (Matthew 13:27, *NIV*)

This is a negative dream.

If you see weeds in a dream, do not underestimate this; face it, or it will be problematic.

To dream of weeds in your garden symbolises hindrances that can easily be taken care of. There is a need to face your responsibilities either at home or at work and take care of issues that, whilst small, are still there.

WEEPING

See **CRIES**

WELL

This dream is a mixed bag.

If you see a full well and you have access to it, it could mean that provisions have been made for you.

It could also mean that you will find help in your time of need, as the Scripture says:

> **"for out of that well they watered the flocks"** (Genesis 29:1–2).

On the other hand, if the well is empty, it shows there is no need to waste your time on a matter or issue you are considering.

WHISPERING

This is a negative dream.

If you see people whispering, it could mean that they are sharing wicked news or information about you. As the psalmist said:

> **"All that hate me whisper together against me: against me do they devise my hurt"** (Psalm 41:7).

If you are among those whispering, it is a warning to desist from gossip that may come back to affect your success.

PSALM 41:7

Decree and declare that all those conspiring and devising against you will never live to execute their plans; decree that their evil imaginations and plans have forever failed and backfired unto them, in Jesus' Name.

WHITE

See **COLOUR**

WILL (TESTAMENT)

Generally, writing a will in a dream shows that you are not at peace with people close to you concerning something that you are handling or about to handle. As the Scripture says:

> **"For where a testament is, there must also of necessity be the death of the testator. For a testament is of force after men are dead: otherwise it is of no strength at all while the testator liveth"** (Hebrews 9:16–17).

WIND

This dream could go either way.

A calm wind in the dream signifies peace and quiet in your dwelling or workplace. Genesis 8:1 says:

> **"God made a wind to pass over the earth, and the waters asswaged."**

If you dream of a violent wind or whirlwind, it could mean that you should expect strong opposition to your endeavours. Like in the book of Exodus 10:13:

> **"the LORD brought an east wind upon the land all that day, and all that night; and when it was morning, the east wind brought the locusts."**

EXODUS 10:13

Prayer Point

Use the Name and the Blood of Jesus to come against any opposition or projection of calamity that has been set against you; command calamity to return back to those who are projecting it, in Jesus' Name.

WINDOW

This dream could either be positive or negative.

An open window indicates that a vital opportunity may come your way but you may underestimate it, for the Word of God says:

> **"if I will not open you the windows of heaven, and pour you out a blessing, that there shall not be room enough to receive it"** (Malachi 3:10).

A closed window indicates that you underrated an opportunity that ought to have been significant.

If your window is smashed or broken, it signifies attempted attacks against your secured position.

WITCH/WIZARD

A witch or wizard in the dream is evil personified against your blessing. God has exposed the strong man or woman in your life and you need to bind them, for the Bible says:

> **"Thou shalt not suffer a witch to live"** (Exodus 22:18).

PSALM 11:3

Use the Name and the Blood of Jesus to separate yourself from every foundation of witchcraft or wizardry that may be operating in your life and hindering God's ordination for you, in Jesus' Name.

MICAH 5:12; MATTHEW 12:29

Use the Name and the Blood of Jesus to bind and paralyse any spirit of witchcraft or wizardry operating against you, your family, your blessings, your finances, etc, in Jesus' Name.

EXODUS 22:18

Decree and declare that any witch or wizard assigned against you and your family will never live to execute their plans; let the Angels of God execute God's judgment upon them, in Jesus' Name.

WOODS (AS IN PLACE)

If you dream of hiding or being alone in the woods, it could mean that you want to escape from reality. You are in denial and are not being honest with yourself over the issues before you.

WOOD (AS IN MATERIAL)

To see yourself carrying wood in your vehicle or on your head in a dream speaks of the efforts you have expended on an issue will yield nothing.

PSALM 128:2

Decree and declare that you will never labour in vain and that the works of your hand shall yield good fruit, in Jesus' Name.

PSALM 78:46

Bind and paralyse any power that wants to frustrate your efforts and that wants to cause you to labour in vain; all those that want to cause you to labour in vain will never live to execute their plans, in Jesus' Name.

WREATH

If you are carrying a wreath, it is a negative dream. You need to cancel the spirit of death assigned to you or your beloved ones immediately.

Prayer: See prayers on BEREAVEMENT.

WRESTLING

This shows that you are determined not to give up on something, despite strong opposition. In the Bible, Jacob wrestled with an angel, and despite being injured, he persisted and eventually the Lord blessed him (Genesis 32:25–29).

It could also indicate that nothing can stop you from achieving your goals.

WRITING

To dream of writing could indicate the seriousness of a matter before you and symbolises your efforts to ensure that things are done correctly, as in when Zacharias was mute and decided to write his son's name "John" (Luke 1:59–63). It shows your determination to seek justice.

Y

YACHT

Dreaming of yachts symbolises luxury or abundance in the fast lane, with all its attendant risks.

YAM

Generally, if you see yams in a dream, it indicates that all your efforts will be fruitful.

DEUTERONOMY 28:5, 8

Prayer Point

> **Thank God for blessing the works of your hands and for allowing your efforts to be fruitful; decree and declare that the fruitfulness God has ordained for you must surely come to pass,** in Jesus' Name.

YAWN

From my own understanding, to yawn in the dream could mean you have resigned yourself to fate over a personal issue.

YELLOW

From my own perspective, yellow in the dream speaks of the power of attraction.

YIELD

See **HARVEST**

YOKE

This is a negative dream.

If you feel you are under a yoke in a dream, it could mean that your life is being controlled and manipulated by forces above you. There is a need to seek spiritual help from an anointed man or woman, for the Word of God says:

> **"and the yoke shall be destroyed because of the anointing"** (Isaiah 10:27).

Prayer Point

1 KINGS 12:11, ISAIAH 10:27

Every yoke of affliction, sickness, poverty, spiritual bondage, etc., that been placed upon your life, or emanating from your foundation, use the Name and the Blood of Jesus to break those yokes and to separate yourself from them, in Jesus' Name.

YOUTH

As the psalmist said:

> **"Bless the LORD, O my soul… Who satisfieth thy mouth with good things; so that thy youth is renewed like the eagle's"**
> (Psalm 103:1–5).

If an old person sees him or herself as young in a dream, it symbolises renewal of strength, health, condition, etc.

Z

ZENITH

Generally, this is a positive dream.

If you are on a pinnacle in a dream, it shows that your personal efforts will take you to higher places.

Prayer: See prayers on TOWER.

ZOO

From my own perspective, if you find yourself in a zoo around wild beasts, this speaks of vulnerability. If care is not taken, the outcome of whatever you are doing may affect your life and your general welfare.

Prayer Point

PROVERBS 3:5—6; PSALM 125:1—2

Pray that God will order your steps and actions so that they will not come back to affect you negatively; pray that God will ever surround you and your family members, and all your endeavours, all the days of your lives, in Jesus' Name.

OTHER RESOURCES BY THE AUTHOR

I believe this book has been a blessing to you, bringing to your life new insights and knowledge. To continually receive such revelational messages, I entreat you to get a copy of the following resources the Lord has graced me to write and your life will surely be blessed:

Why Die Before Your Time?

Earth as a Weapon of Defence or Warfare

The Heavenlies

The Blood of Jesus as a Weapon

The Water Realm

Overthrowing Evil Altars

In addition to these, there are several DVD messages available to purchase on the church's website: www.jesussanctuaryministries.org.

May the Lord grant you understanding as you enrich yourself in the knowledge of God.